**EXPLORE
SUDAN**

THE TREASURE

الكنز

EXPLORE SUDAN

Copyright © 2021 Explore Sudan

All rights reserved.

No part of this publication may be reproduced, distributed, or transmitted in any form or by any means, including photocopying, recording, or other electronic or mechanical methods, without express written permission of the author.

Images are for illustration purposes only.

Maps are not drawn to scale.

EXPLORE SUDAN

"نحن بمقاييس العالم الصناعي الأوروبي، فلاحون فقراء، ولكنني حين أعانق جدي أحس بالغنى، كأنني نغمة من دقات قلب الكون نفسه."

الطيب الصالح

"By the standards of the European industrial world we are poor peasants, but when I embrace my grandfather I experience a sense of richness as though I am a note in the heartbeats of the very universe."

El-Tayeb Salih

EXPLORE SUDAN

No matter how far we go,

Our parents are the light that shines within us,

An incessant source of inspiration and love.

Dedicated to my dear family and

to my beloved parents,

Prof. Abd El Moneim ElSeed and Fatma ElShazali.

EXPLORE SUDAN

In the next pages there is no mention of war, conflict, or failed governance. Through this skewed perspective, the true potential of Sudan emerges unobscured by its history of political strife.

The perception that resources are scarce is a well-established cause of conflict. Embracing our differences becomes possible once we realize that the homeland we share is far greater than us; that amidst all the chaos lies a country of infinite resources yet to be discovered.

Changing reality begins with a vision. I hope this book encourages new generations to visualize a future Sudan that centers on abundance, prosperity, and equity. Sudan's most valuable resource is not petrol or gold, it is the love and patriotism of its children.

Nouar ElSaid

EXPLORE SUDAN

Darfur Region (Pg 16)	**Kordofan Region** (Pg 22)	**Northern State** (Pg 28)
River Nile State (Pg 32)	**Red Sea State** (Pg 38)	**Kassala State** (Pg 44)

EXPLORE SUDAN

Al-Gadarif State — Pg 48	**Al-Gezirah State** — Pg 52	**Sennar State** — Pg 56
White Nile State — Pg 62	**Blue Nile State** — Pg 66	**Khartoum State** — Pg 70

Overview of Sudan's Resources — Pg 80

EXPLORE SUDAN

Maps

SUDAN LOCATION

موقع السودان

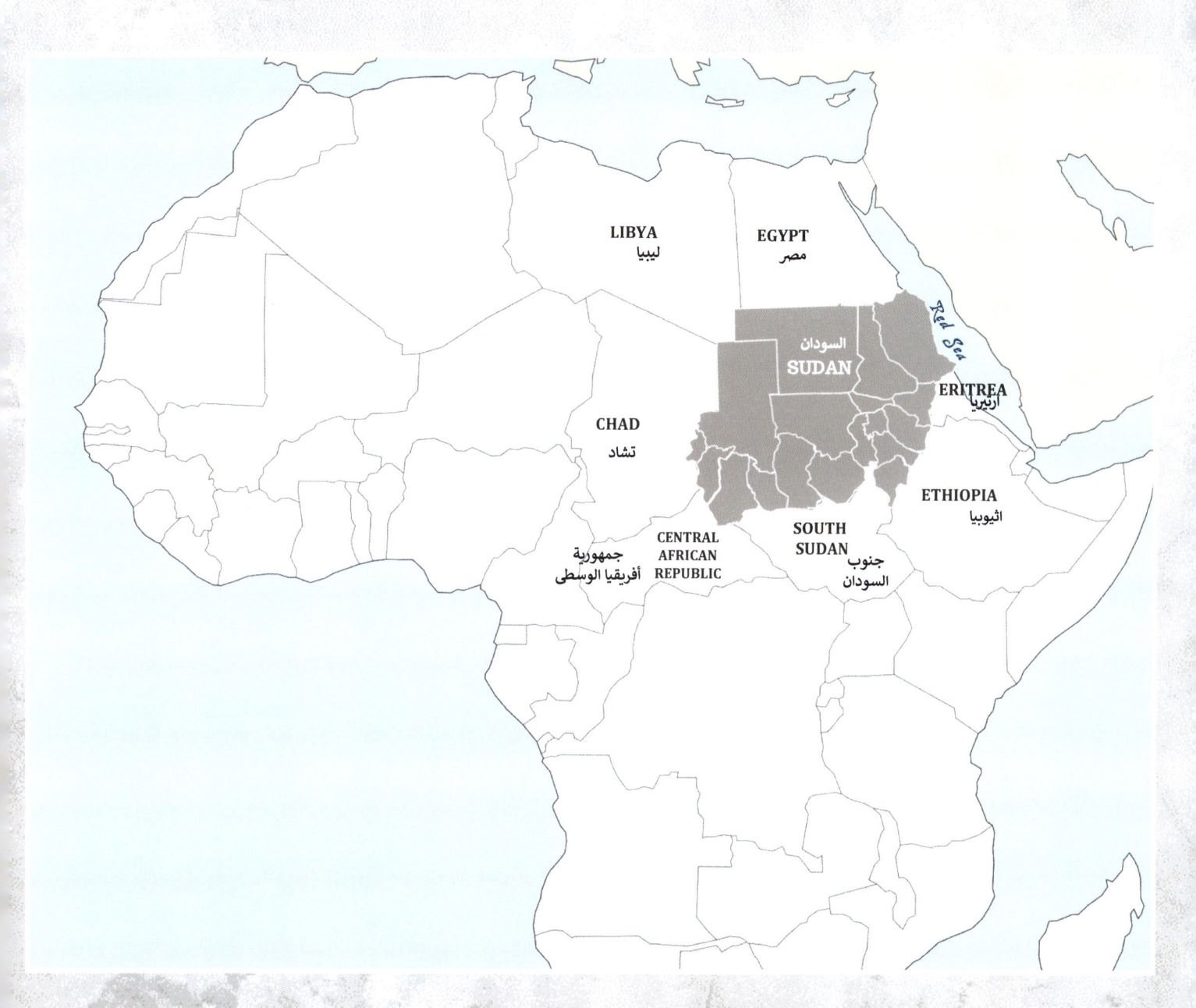

SUDAN STATES

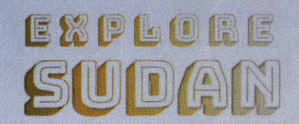

ولايات السودان

Key	State	State Capital
ND	North Darfur	AlFasher
WD	West Darfur	El Geneina
CD	Central Darfur	Zaleingei
SD	South Darfur	Nyala
ED	East Darfur	Ad-dein
NK	North Kordofan	ElObied
WK	West Kordofan	AlFula
SK	South Kordofan	Kadogli
NS	Northern State	Dongola
RN	River Nile	Ad-damer
RS	Red Sea	Port-Sudan
KS	Kassala	Kassala
GZ	Al-Gazirah	Al-Gazirah
GD	Al-Gadarif	Al-Gadarif
SN	Sennar	Singa
WN	White Nile	Rabak
BN	Blue Nile	Ad-Damazin
📍	Khartoum	Khartoum

SUDAN STATES

ولايات السودان

SUDAN STATES

ولايات السودان

الرمز	الولاية	العاصمة
ND	ولاية شمال دارفور	الفاشر
WD	ولاية غرب دارفور	الجنينة
CD	ولاية وسط دارفور	زالنجي
SD	ولاية جنوب دارفور	نيالا
ED	ولاية شرق دارفور	الضعين
NK	ولاية شمال كردفان	الأبيض
WK	ولاية غرب كردفان	الفولة
SK	ولاية جنوب كردفان	كادوقلي
NS	الولاية الشمالية	دنقلا
RN	ولاية نهر النيل	الدامر
RS	ولاية البحر الأحمر	بورتسودان
KS	ولاية كسلا	كسلا
GZ	ولاية الجزيرة	ود مدني
GD	ولاية القضارف	القضارف
SN	ولاية سنار	سنجة
WN	ولاية النيل الأبيض	ربك
BN	ولاية النيل الأزرق	الدمازين
📍	ولاية الخرطوم	الخرطوم

SUDAN STATES

ولايات السودان

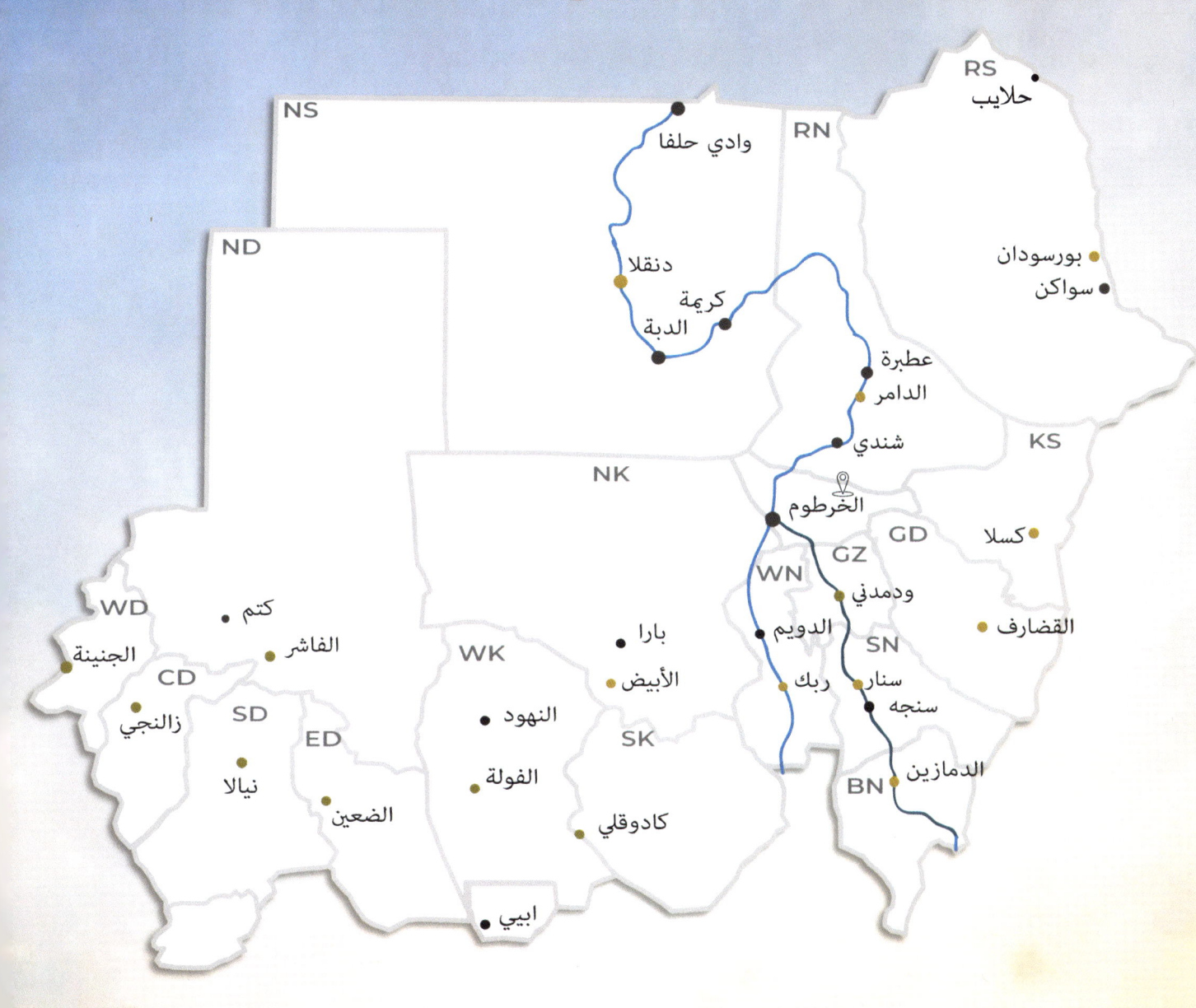

EXPLORE SUDAN

Visual Guide

EXPLORE SUDAN

DARFUR

EXPLORE SUDAN

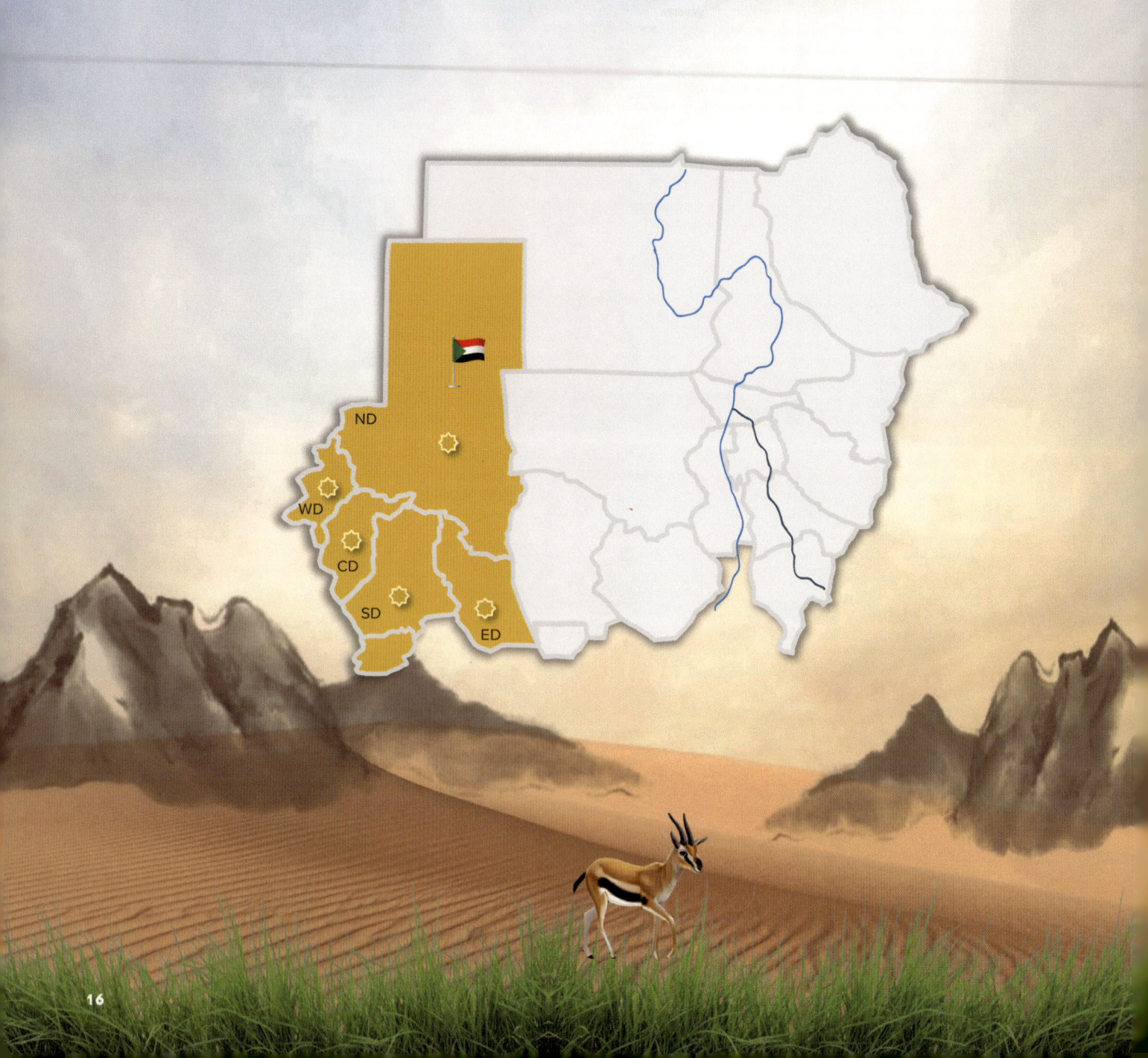

دارفور

ND
WD
CD
SD
ED

DARFUR

دارفور

Darfur lies in western Sudan. The region is divided into 5 administrative states: **North Darfur, South Darfur, East Darfur, West Darfur** and **Central Darfur.** The region of Darfur is approximately the size of Spain. The high volcanic mountains of **Jebel Marrah** are a distinct landmark.

Darfur is rich in many natural resources. It is home to some of Sudan's largest **gold mines** and **mineral reserves**. It is also an important source of **Gum Arabic**, which is a natural product extracted from a tree known as the **Acacia** tree. Gum Arabic is used in many industries and is an important component of many food items and drugs (see page 82).

DARFUR

EXPLORE SUDAN

دارفور

DARFUR — دارفور

Jebel Marrah	جبل مرة
Wadi Howr	وادي هور
Ali Dinar Museum	متحف علي دينار

Gum Arabic	الصمغ العربي
Agriculture	الزراعة
Millet	الدخن
Livestock	الماشية
Gold	الذهب
Minerals	المعادن
Marble	الرخام

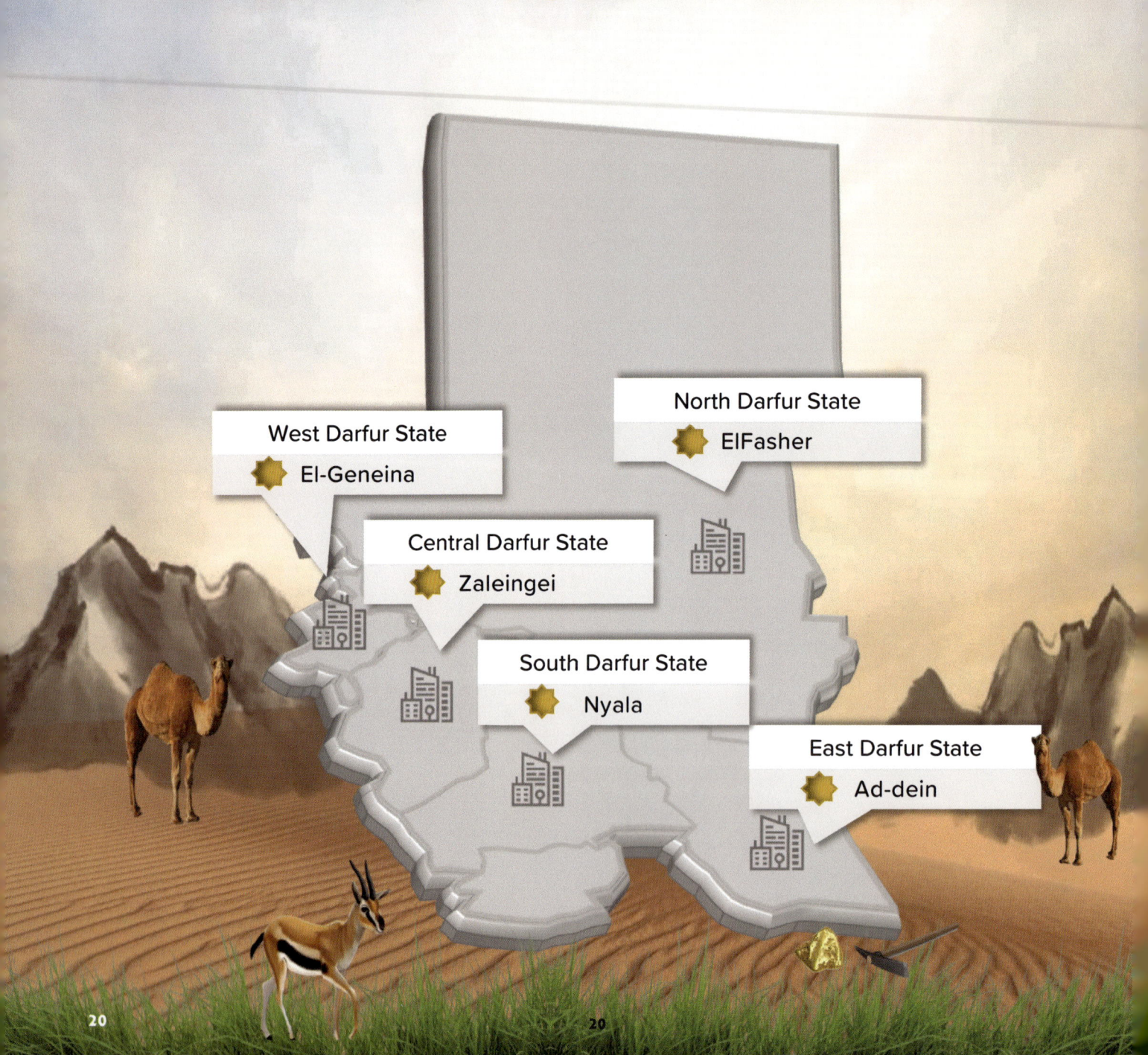

DARFUR

دارفور

West Darfur State — El-Geneina

North Darfur State — ElFasher

Central Darfur State — Zaleingei

South Darfur State — Nyala

East Darfur State — Ad-dein

DARFUR دارفور

Jebel Marrah mountains in Darfur are a set of **volcanic mountains** that extend more than 10,000 feet high. The peak of Jebel Marrah is the highest point in Sudan.

The area of **Wadi Howr** features diverse flora and remarkable geological features. It contains the crater site of **Meidob Hills**, which is a volcanic field. The area is grazed by gazelles, ostriches and other forms of desert wildlife.

Ali Dinar was a former Sultan of the **Sultanate of Darfur**. He is known to have bravely fought against colonialism and died defending his homeland. His house is now a museum.

KORDOFAN

EXPLORE SUDAN

كردفان

NK
WK
SK

KORDOFAN

كردفان

The region of **Kordofan** is divided into three states: **North Kordofan**, **South Kordofan** and **West Kordofan**. The geographic area of Kordofan is marked by the **Nuba Mountains**.

Kordofan is a diverse region that is home to a large group of different tribes. The main activities in **Kordofan** are centered on agriculture and animal breeding.

Some of Sudan's **largest oil fields** are found here, mostly in South Kordofan. Kordofan is also an important source of **Gum Arabic.**

EXPLORE SUDAN

KORDOFAN	كردفان

Nuba Mountains	جبال النوبة

El-Obied Mosque	مسجد الأبيض

Gum Arabic	الصمغ العربي

Livestock	الماشية

Agriculture	الزراعة

Oil Fields	البترول

KORDOFAN — EXPLORE SUDAN — كردفان

The **Nuba Mountains** in **South Kordofan** stretch over 48,000 square kilometers. The capital city of South Kordofan is **Kadugli**.

El-Obied City is the capital of **North Kordofan** state and an important transportation hub. **El-Obied mosque** is one of the landmark locations in the city.

Gum Arabic (Acacia Arabica) is a natural product that is obtained from the sap (fluid) of the **Acacia trees**. Gum Arabic has many uses, most importantly it is used in the food industry (See page 82).

KORDOFAN

كردفان

North Kordofan State
ElObied

West Kordofan State
Al-Fula

South Kordofan State
Kadugli

KORDOFAN

EXPLORE SUDAN

كردفان

The **Kordofan Giraffe** is an endangered species found in many areas in Africa including western Sudan.

NORTHERN STATE

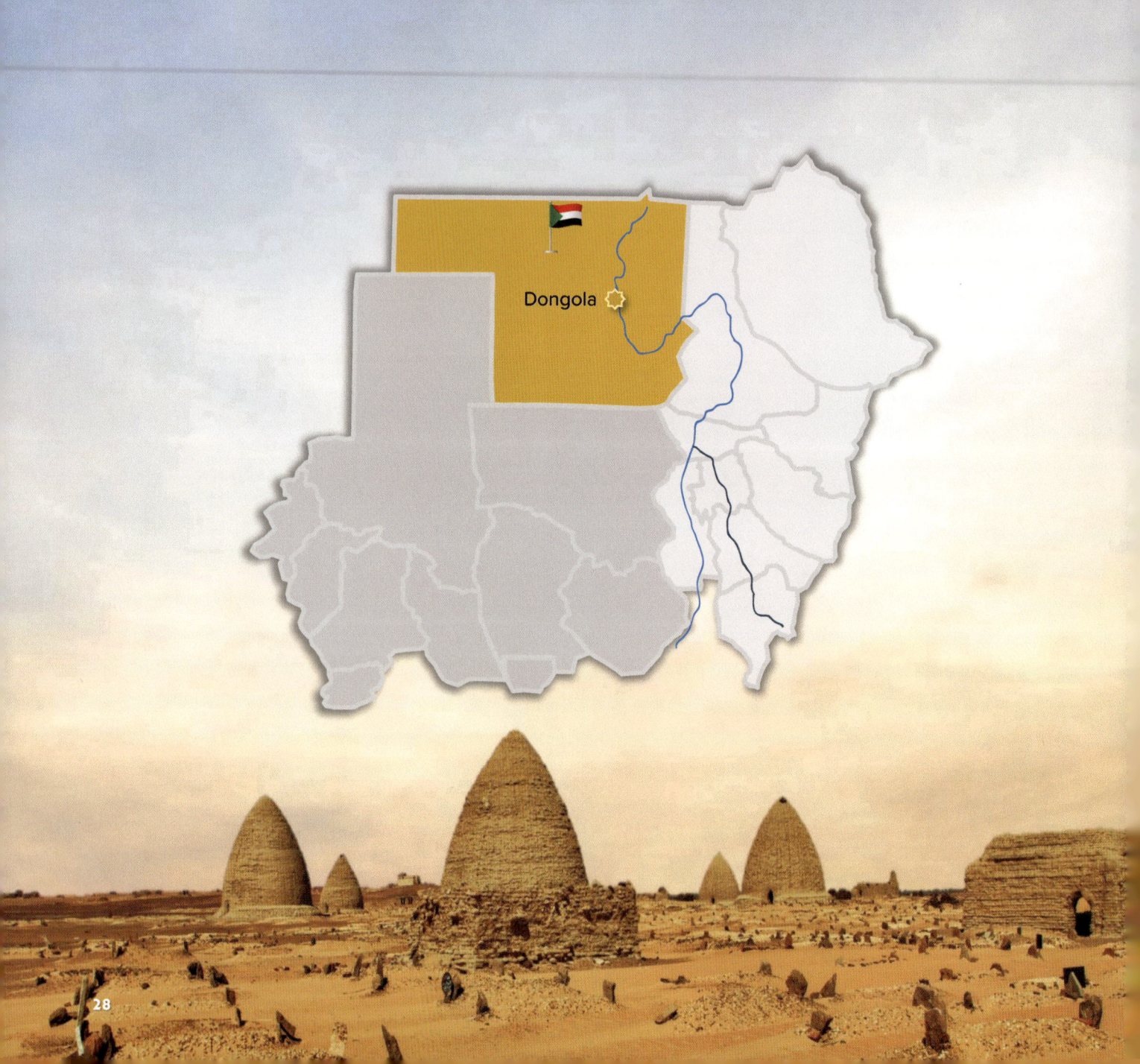

EXPLORE SUDAN

الولاية الشمالية

Dongola

NORTHERN STATE

EXPLORE SUDAN

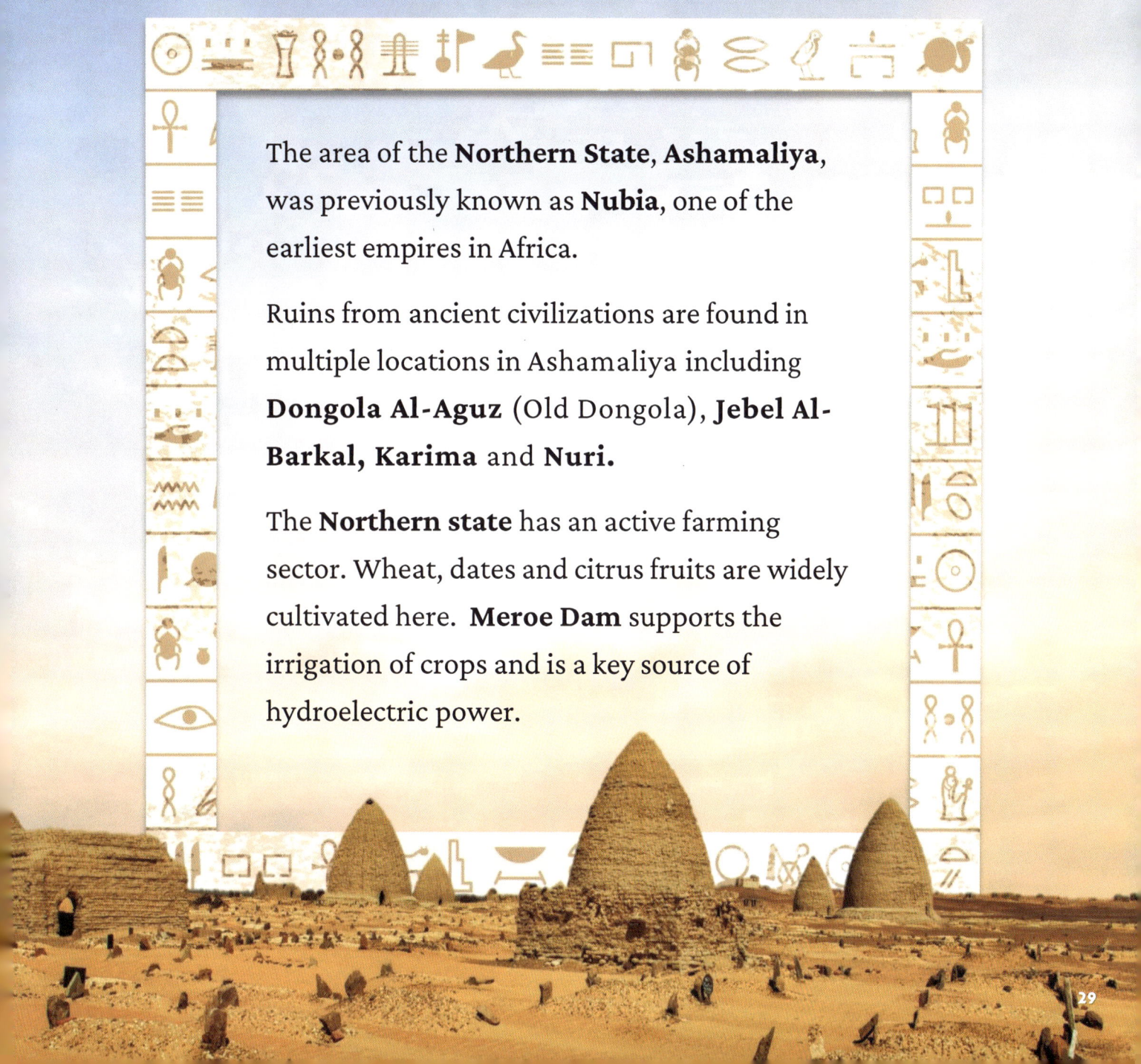

الولاية الشماليه

The area of the **Northern State**, **Ashamaliya**, was previously known as **Nubia**, one of the earliest empires in Africa.

Ruins from ancient civilizations are found in multiple locations in Ashamaliya including **Dongola Al-Aguz** (Old Dongola), **Jebel Al-Barkal, Karima** and **Nuri.**

The **Northern state** has an active farming sector. Wheat, dates and citrus fruits are widely cultivated here. **Meroe Dam** supports the irrigation of crops and is a key source of hydroelectric power.

NORTHERN STATE

EXPLORE SUDAN

الولاية الشماليه

Meroe Dam	خزان مروي
Jebel Barkal	جبل البركل
Nuri	نوري
Old Dongola	دنقلا العجوز

Wheat	القمح
Dates	التمر
Agriculture	الزراعة

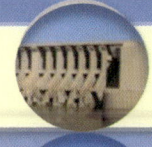

NORTHERN STATE　　　　　　　　　　　الولاية الشماليه

Meroe Dam is one of the largest hydropower projects in Africa. The dam protects the lower Nile valley from floods and is an important source of **hydroelectric power.**

Jebel Barkal is a mountain in **Karima** city. At its base lies the ancient city of **Napta** and the **Pyramids of Jebel Barkal**. The site has ruins from 13 temples and 3 palaces.

Nuri has ancient pyramids marking the locations of the tombs of **Nubian kings and queens.** One of the largest tombs belongs to **Taharqa,** the King of the **Kingdom of Kush.**

Dongola Alaguz or Old Dongola is a town that lies east of the River Nile. It was the capital of the ancient Nubian '**Kingdom of Dongola**' or '**Makuria.**' Ruins from the previous era remain standing until today.

RIVER NILE STATE

EXPLORE SUDAN

ولاية نهر النيل

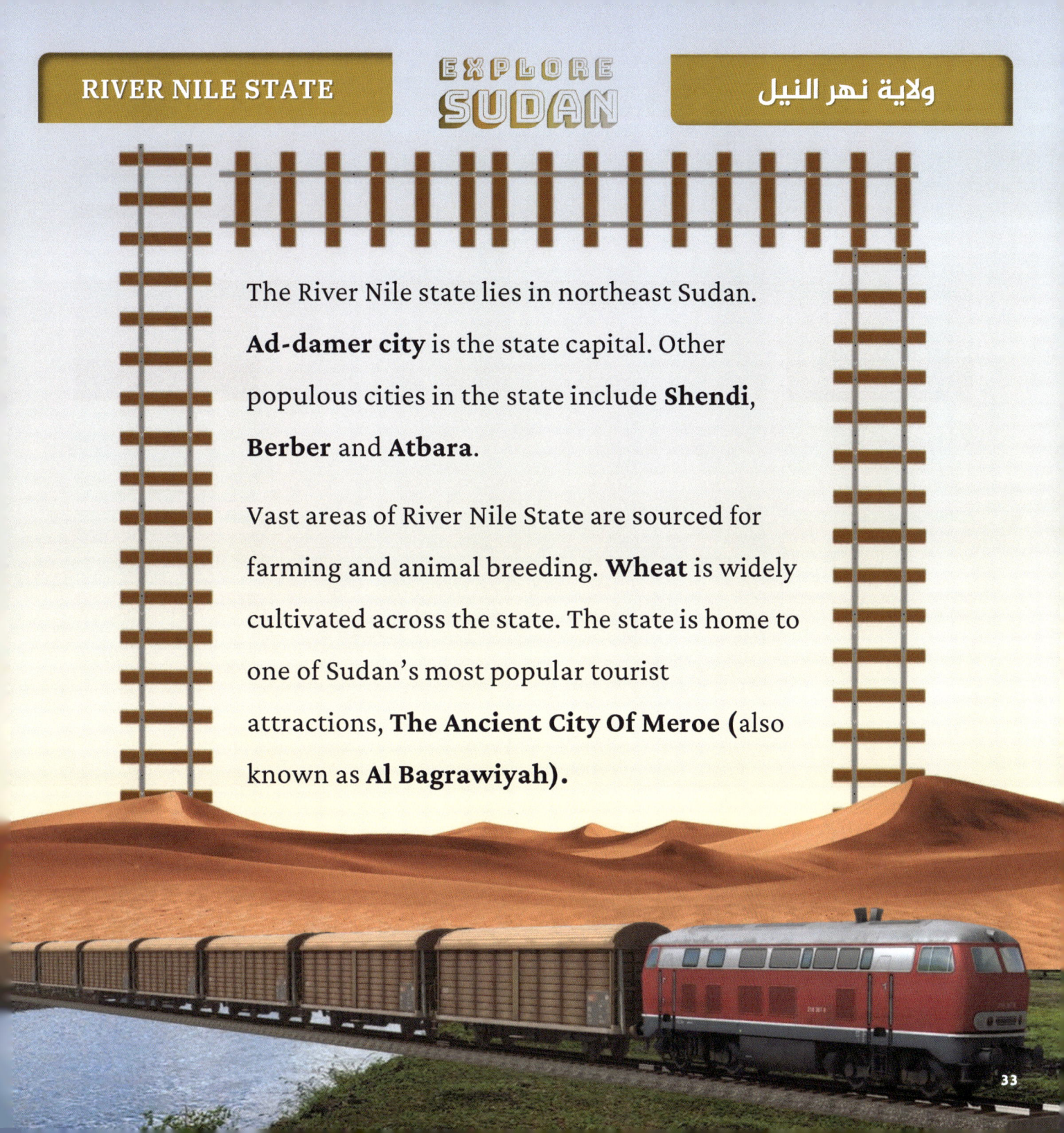

RIVER NILE STATE

ولاية نهر النيل

The River Nile state lies in northeast Sudan. **Ad-damer city** is the state capital. Other populous cities in the state include **Shendi**, **Berber** and **Atbara**.

Vast areas of River Nile State are sourced for farming and animal breeding. **Wheat** is widely cultivated across the state. The state is home to one of Sudan's most popular tourist attractions, **The Ancient City Of Meroe (**also known as **Al Bagrawiyah).**

EXPLORE SUDAN

RIVER NILE STATE		ولاية نهر النيل
Al Bagrawiyah		البجراوية
Atbara River		نهر عطبرة
Bayuda Desert		صحراء بيوضة
Railway		السكة حديد
Cement		أسمنت عطبرة
Wheat		القمح
Livestock		الماشية

34

RIVER NILE STATE

EXPLORE SUDAN

ولاية نهر النيل

Atbara River is one of the largest tributaries of the River Nile. It rises in **Ethiopia** and travels to north **Sudan** to join the **River Nile** in the city of Atbara.

The headquarters of **Sudan's National railway** is located in **Atbara city.** Atbara is an important commercial and agricultural center. It also houses Sudan's largest **cement** manufacturing companies.

Bayuda Desert lies between the Nubian and Northern deserts, within the great bend of the Nile. It is known for its intriguing geological features, especially the **Bayuda volcanic field** which has remnants from prehistoric volcanic activity.

| AL BAGRAWIYAH | EXPLORE SUDAN | البجراوية |

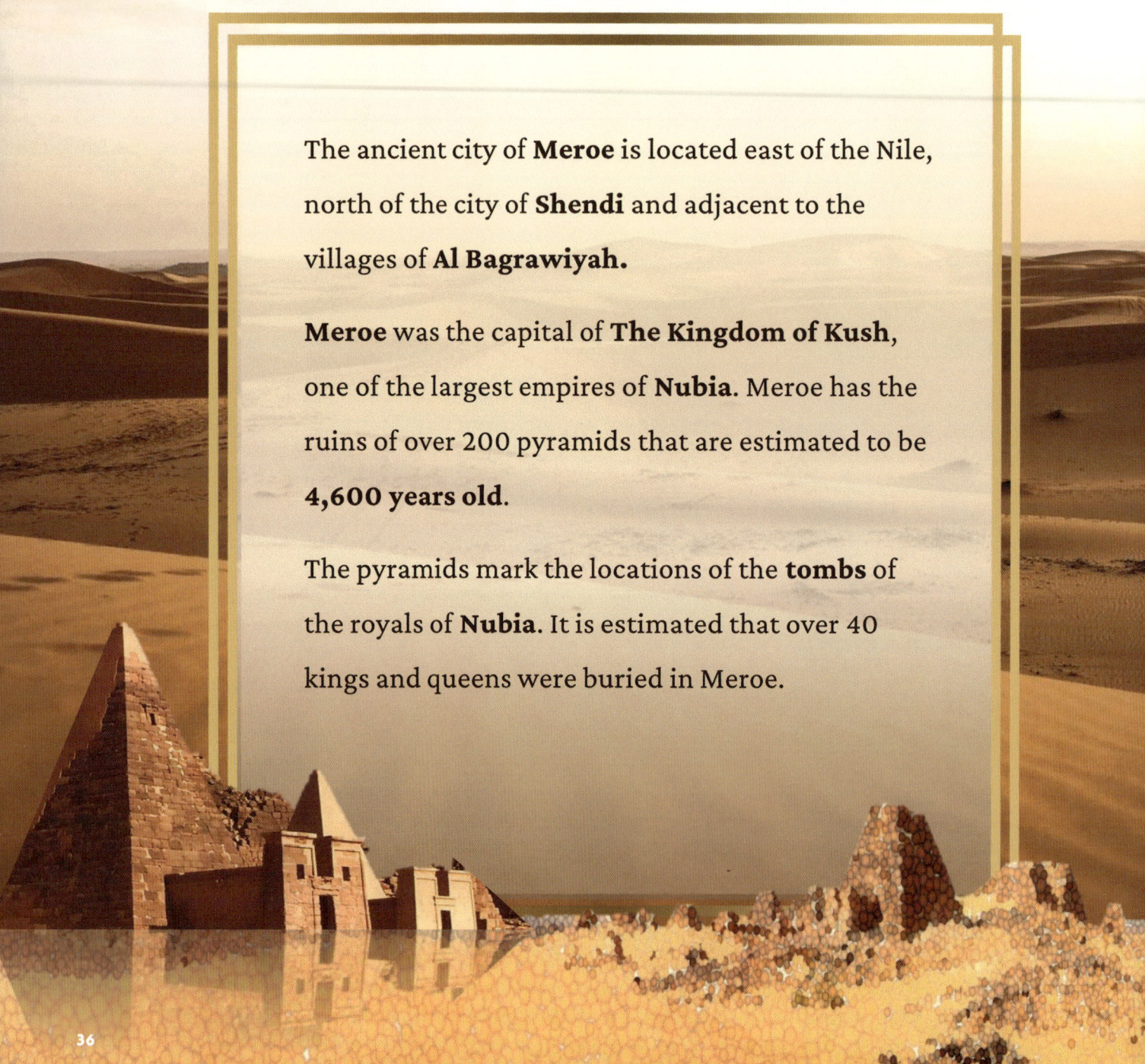

The ancient city of **Meroe** is located east of the Nile, north of the city of **Shendi** and adjacent to the villages of **Al Bagrawiyah**.

Meroe was the capital of **The Kingdom of Kush**, one of the largest empires of **Nubia**. Meroe has the ruins of over 200 pyramids that are estimated to be **4,600 years old**.

The pyramids mark the locations of the **tombs** of the royals of **Nubia**. It is estimated that over 40 kings and queens were buried in Meroe.

BAYUDA DESERT

EXPLORE SUDAN

صحراء بيوضة

This is an image of **Bayuda volcanic field**, which lies at the center of the **Bayuda desert** in northeast Sudan. The image shows the remnants of lava flows from a volcanic eruption that occurred almost 1,100 years ago.

Image credit: NASA Space Shuttle image ISS004-711-20, 200 (http://eol.jsc.nasa.gov/).

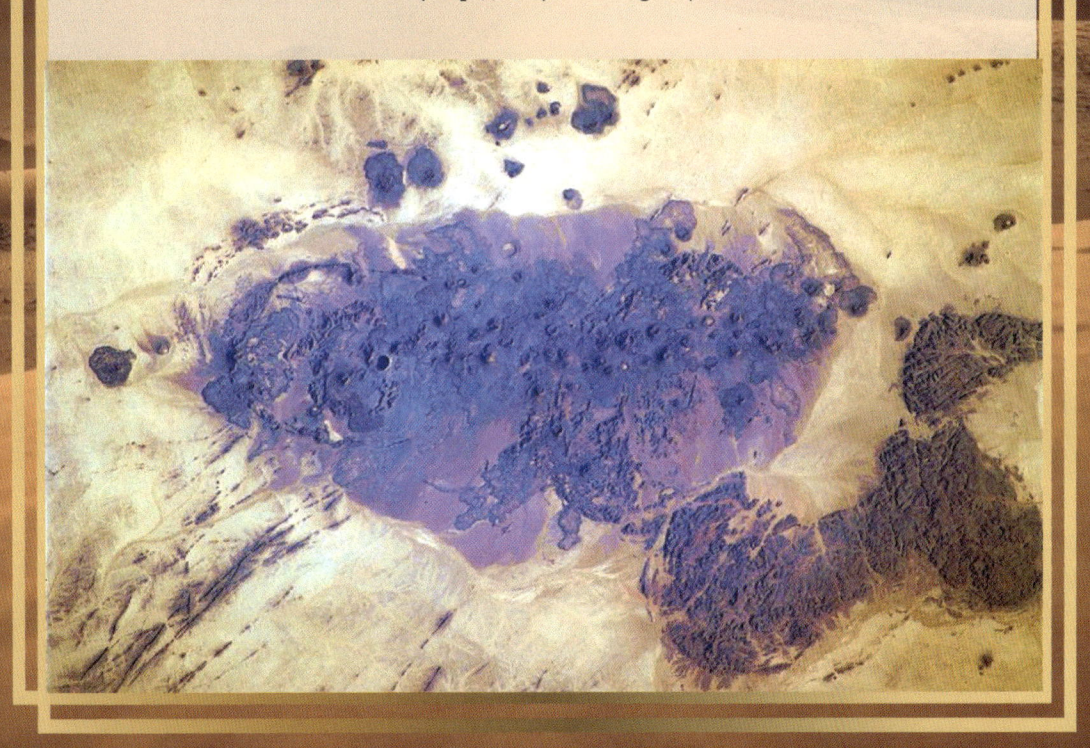

RED SEA STATE

ولاية البحر الأحمر

Port Sudan
Sawakin

| RED SEA STATE | ولاية البحر الأحمر |

The **Red Sea State** lies in northeastern Sudan. **Port-Sudan**, the state capital, is located on the coast of the **Red Sea**. **Port-Sudan** is Sudan's central port while the city of **Sawakin** is the secondary port.

The area of the **Red Sea** adjacent to Sudan's coast contains magnificent **coral reefs** and remarkable marine life.

Port Sudan, Dungonab Bay, Mukkawar Island and **Sanganeb** are popular tourist destinations.

RED SEA STATE

EXPLORE SUDAN

ولاية البحر الأحمر

RED SEA STATE		ولاية البحر الأحمر	
Port-Sudan	بورسودان	Oil Refinery	مصفاة البترول
Sawakin	سواكن	Agriculture	الزراعة
Sanganeeb	سنقنيب	Fisheries	مصائد الأسماك
Coral Reef	شعب مرجانية	Gold	الذهب

41

| RED SEA STATE | EXPLORE SUDAN | ولاية البحر الأحمر |

Port Sudan city is the center for Sudan's international export and import operations. It is equipped with modern **docking facilities** and a **petrol refinery**.

Sawakin is Sudan's second **port** city. In medieval times, it was the central entryway for pilgrims heading to Saudi Arabia, primarily travelers coming from the western parts of the African continent. **Sawakin** lies amidst dense coral reefs.

Dungonab Bay and **Mukkawar Island** are located north of Port Sudan. They are home to one of the most diverse marine ecosystems in the world, featuring stunning **coral reefs** and **beaches**.

Sanganeb is the only **atoll** (ring-shaped coral reef island) in the Red Sea. It is known for its **biodiversity** featuring **13 coral reef zones** and over **300 fish species**.

RED SEA STATE

ولاية البحر الأحمر

- Bottlenose Dolphins
- Humpback Whales
- Hammerhead Sharks
- Hawksbill Turtles

KASSALA STATE

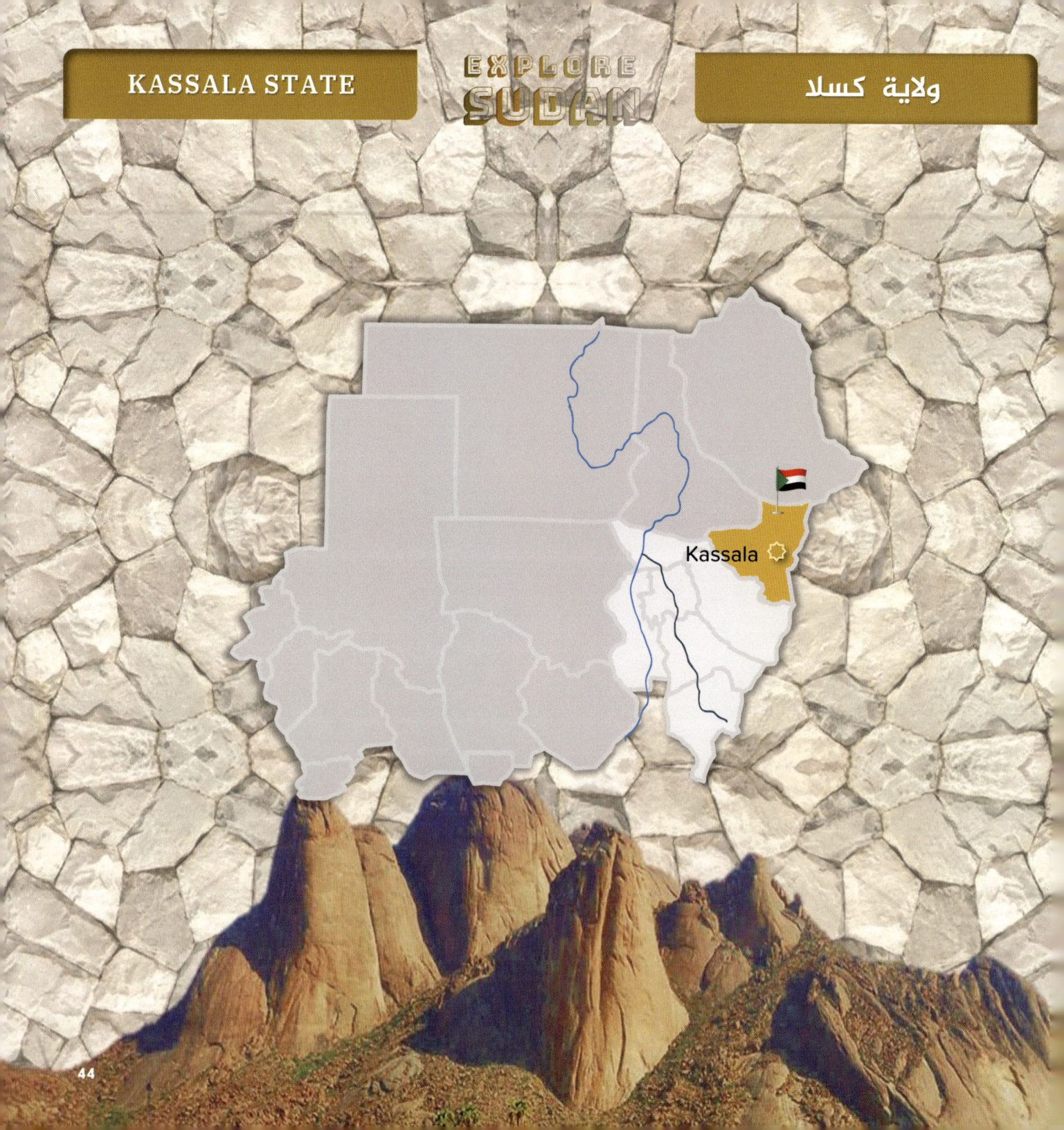

ولاية كسلا

Kassala

KASSALA STATE

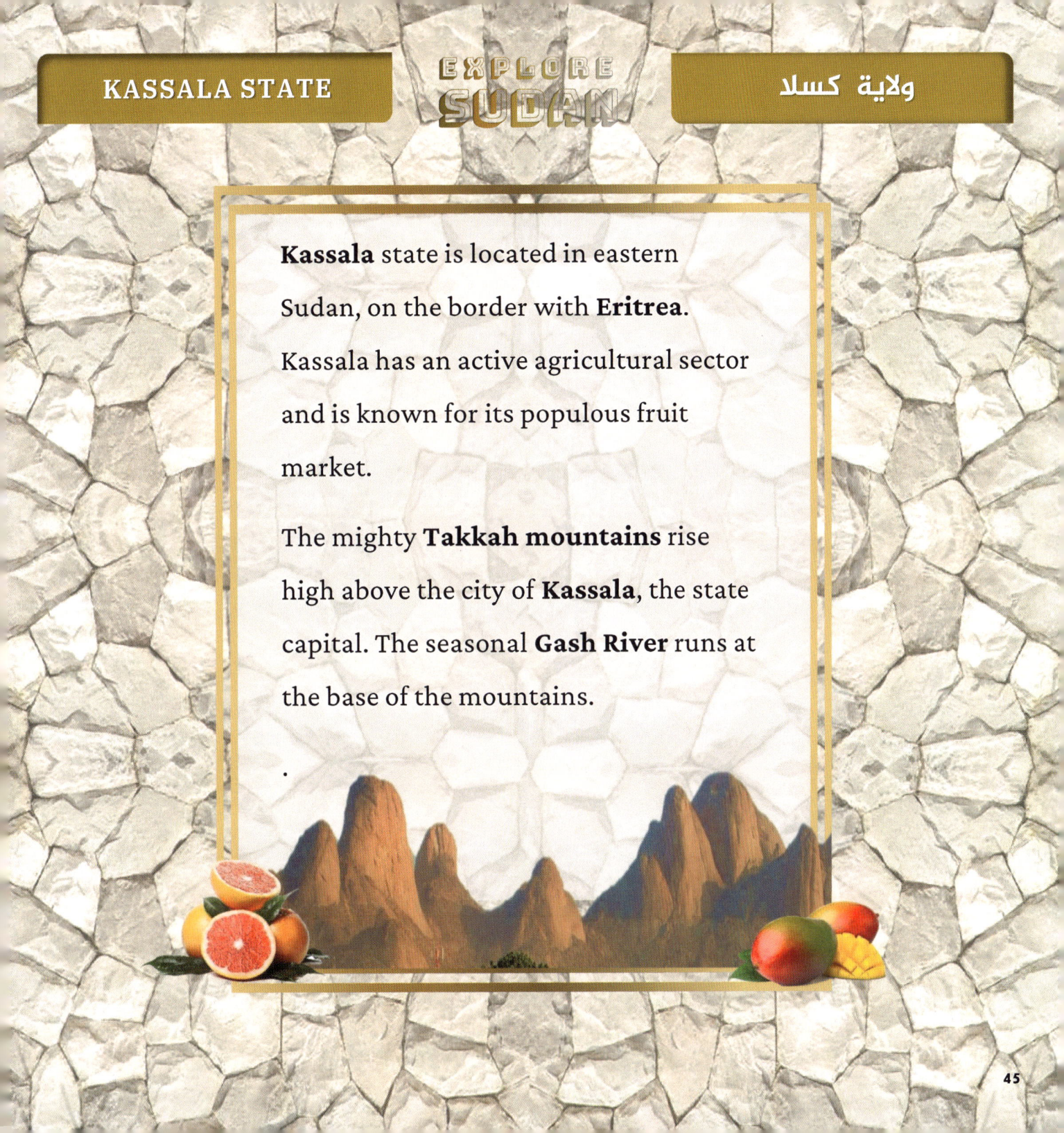

ولاية كسلا

Kassala state is located in eastern Sudan, on the border with **Eritrea**. Kassala has an active agricultural sector and is known for its populous fruit market.

The mighty **Takkah mountains** rise high above the city of **Kassala**, the state capital. The seasonal **Gash River** runs at the base of the mountains.

KASSALA STATE

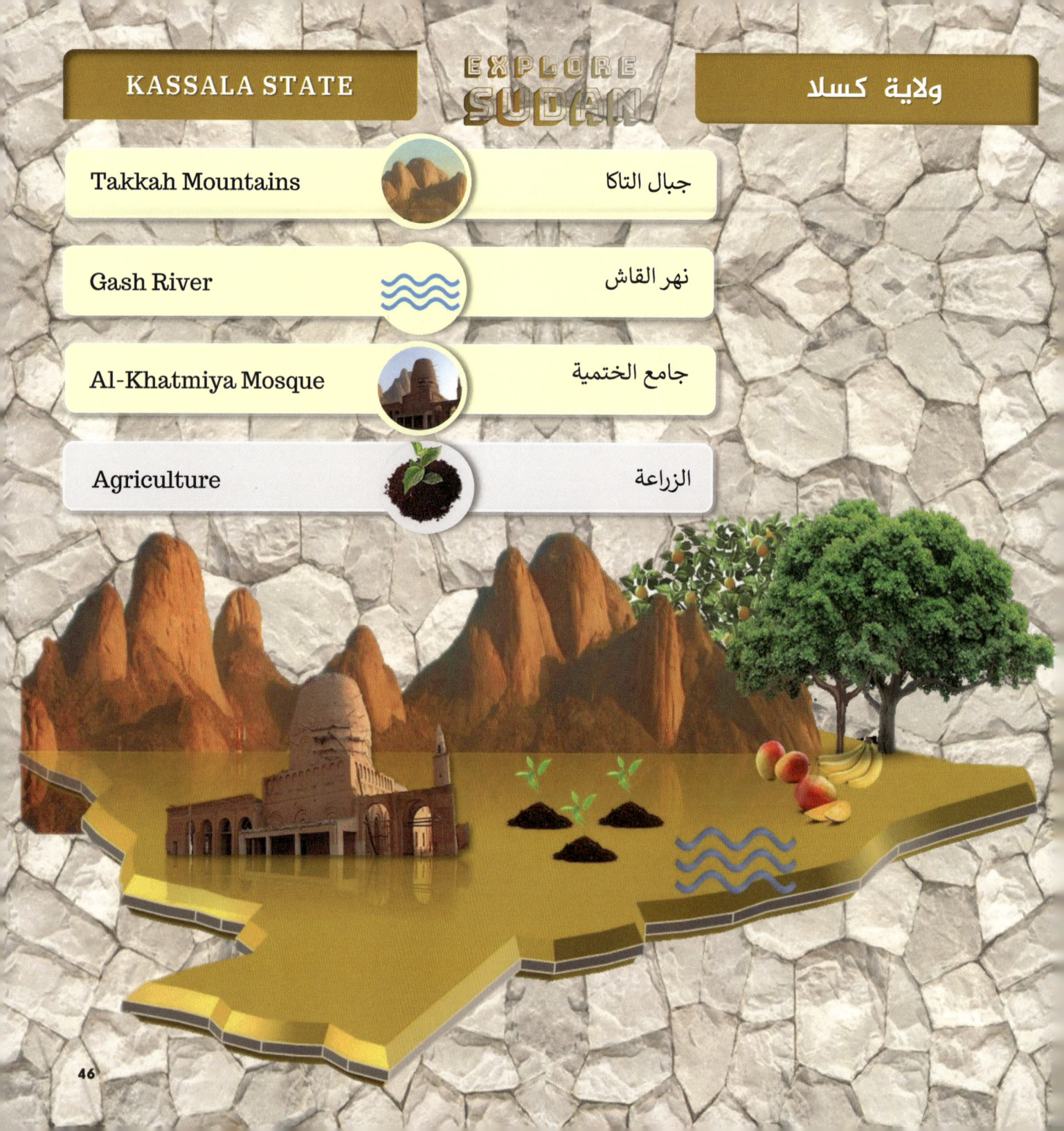

ولاية كسلا

Takkah Mountains	جبال التاكا
Gash River	نهر القاش
Al-Khatmiya Mosque	جامع الختمية
Agriculture	الزراعة

KASSALA STATE

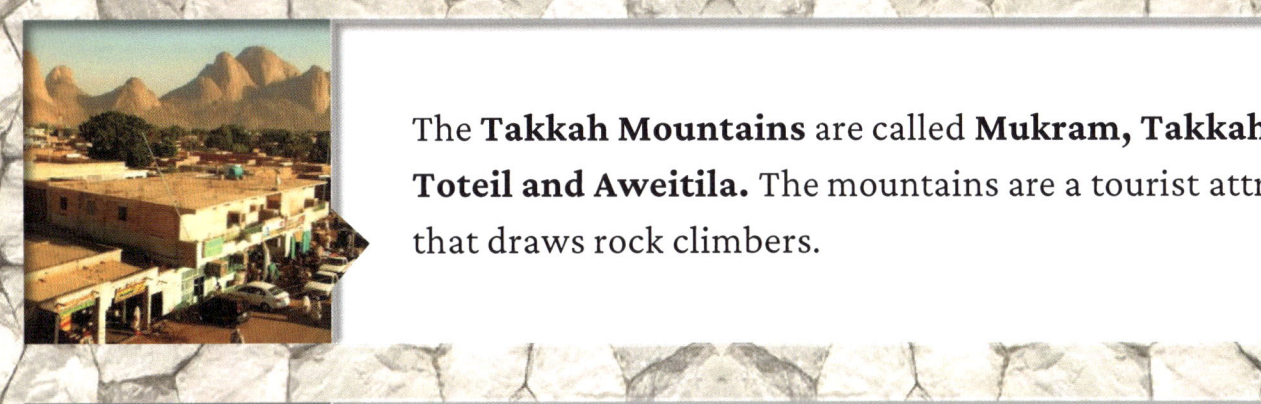

ولاية كسلا

The **Takkah Mountains** are called **Mukram, Takkah, Toteil and Aweitila.** The mountains are a tourist attraction that draws rock climbers.

The **Gash River** rises in **Eritrea** where it is known as the **Mareb** River. It runs through **Sudan** to reach the base of the **Takkah mountains**. It is a **seasonal** river, so it's dry most of the year but may flood during the rainy season.

Al-Khatmiya mosque is located at the base of the Takkah mountains. The mosque is central to the **Khatmiyah Sufi order** in Sudan.

AL-GADARIF STATE

ولاية القضارف

AL-GADARIF STATE

ولاية القضارف

Al-Gadarif state is located in eastern **Sudan**, on the border with **Ethiopia**. Some of the largest **agricultural projects** in Sudan are located in Al-Gadarif, where the land is fertile and rainfall is abundant. A wide variety of crops are cultivated here including **sunflower**, **sesame**, **sorghum**, **fruits**, **okra**, **maize** and **lemons**.

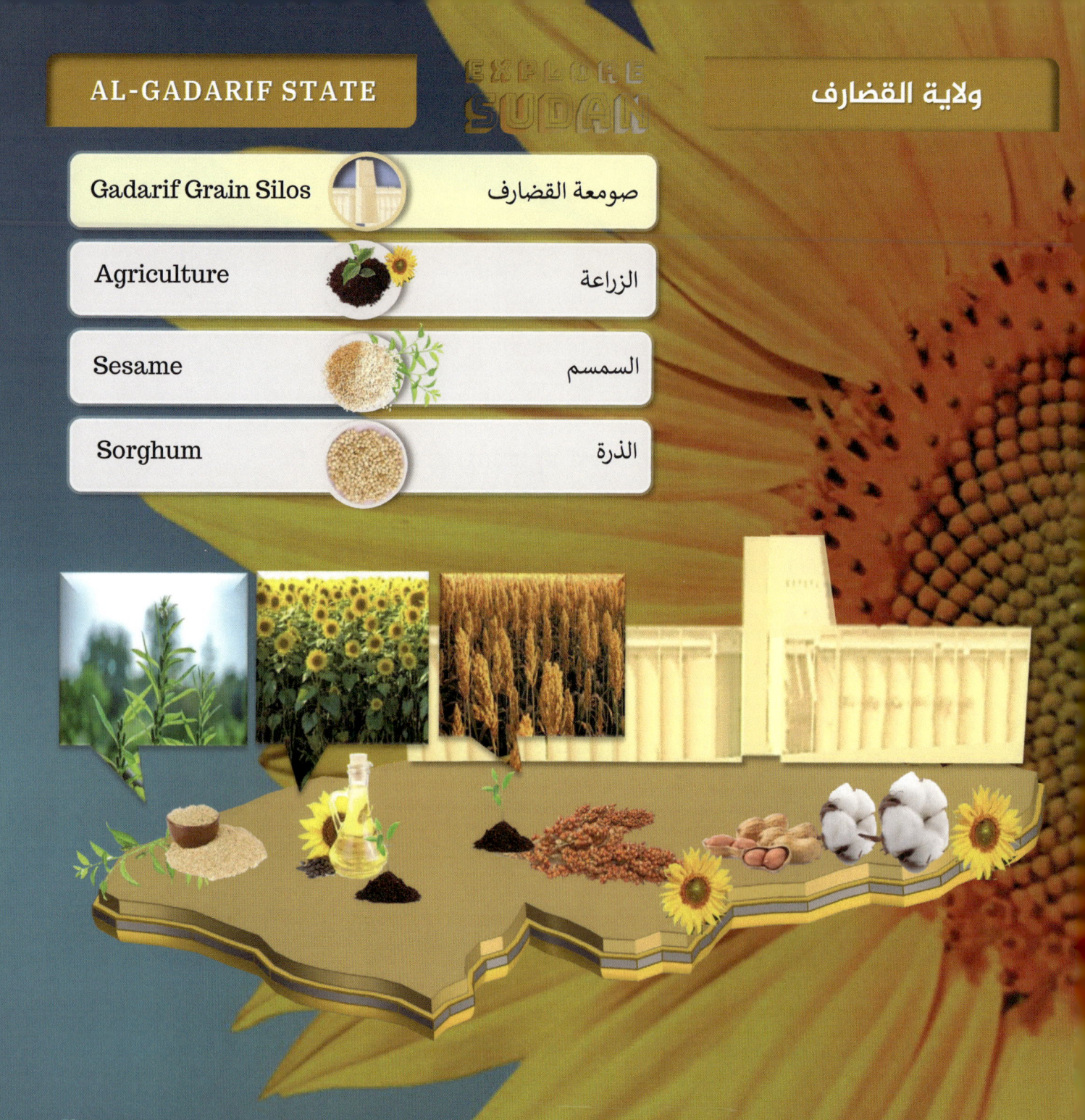

AL-GADARIF STATE

ولاية القضارف

Gadarif Grain Silos	صومعة القضارف
Agriculture	الزراعة
Sesame	السمسم
Sorghum	الذرة

50

AL-GADARIF STATE

ولاية القضارف

One of the distinct features of **Al–Gadarif** is the large **grain silos** that are used to store grains. Al-Gadarif State is a **trade center** for various products including seeds, sesame, cereals, peanuts and sunflower.

Sorghum is a particularly important crop in Sudan since it is used to make **Kisra**, the Sudanese staple food.

Sesame is traded on a wide scale in Al-Gadarif. This has been reflected in **Sudanese folklore** and songs which refer to "**Simsim Al-Gadarif**" ie Al-Gadarif sesame.

AL-GEZIRAH STATE

EXPLORE SUDAN

ولاية الجزيرة

Wad Madani

AL-GEZIRAH STATE

ولاية الجزيرة

"**Gezirah**" in Arabic means island or peninsula and is used to refer to the area between the two **Niles** as they head towards **Khartoum**.

The state is home to **The Gezirah Irrigation Scheme**, one of the largest irrigation schemes in the world. Although many areas of **Sudan** are cultivated, the scheme benefits from the use of advanced machinery to boost crop production. Al-Gezirah is a principal source of **wheat** and **cotton** in Sudan.

AL-GEZIRAH STATE

ولاية الجزيرة

Al-Gezirah University	جامعة الجزيرة
Al Gezirah Scheme	مشروع الجزيرة
Livestock	الماشية
Agriculture	الزراعة

AL-GEZIRAH STATE

ولاية الجزيرة

Al Gezirah Irrigation Scheme is one of the largest irrigation schemes in the world. It centers on the production of cotton, wheat, sorghum, groundnuts, and vegetables.

Al Gezirah University is a leading public university founded in 1975. It is the first university established outside Khartoum and spans across 6 campuses.

Wad Madani, the capital of **Al Gezirah**, is the birth home of many distinguished Sudanese musicians including Mohamed El Amin and Ibrahim El-Kashef. The renowned singer and composer, Mustafa Seed Ahmed, was born in Wad Sulfab village, also in **Al Gezirah.**

SENNAR STATE

EXPLORE SUDAN

ولاية سنار

Singa

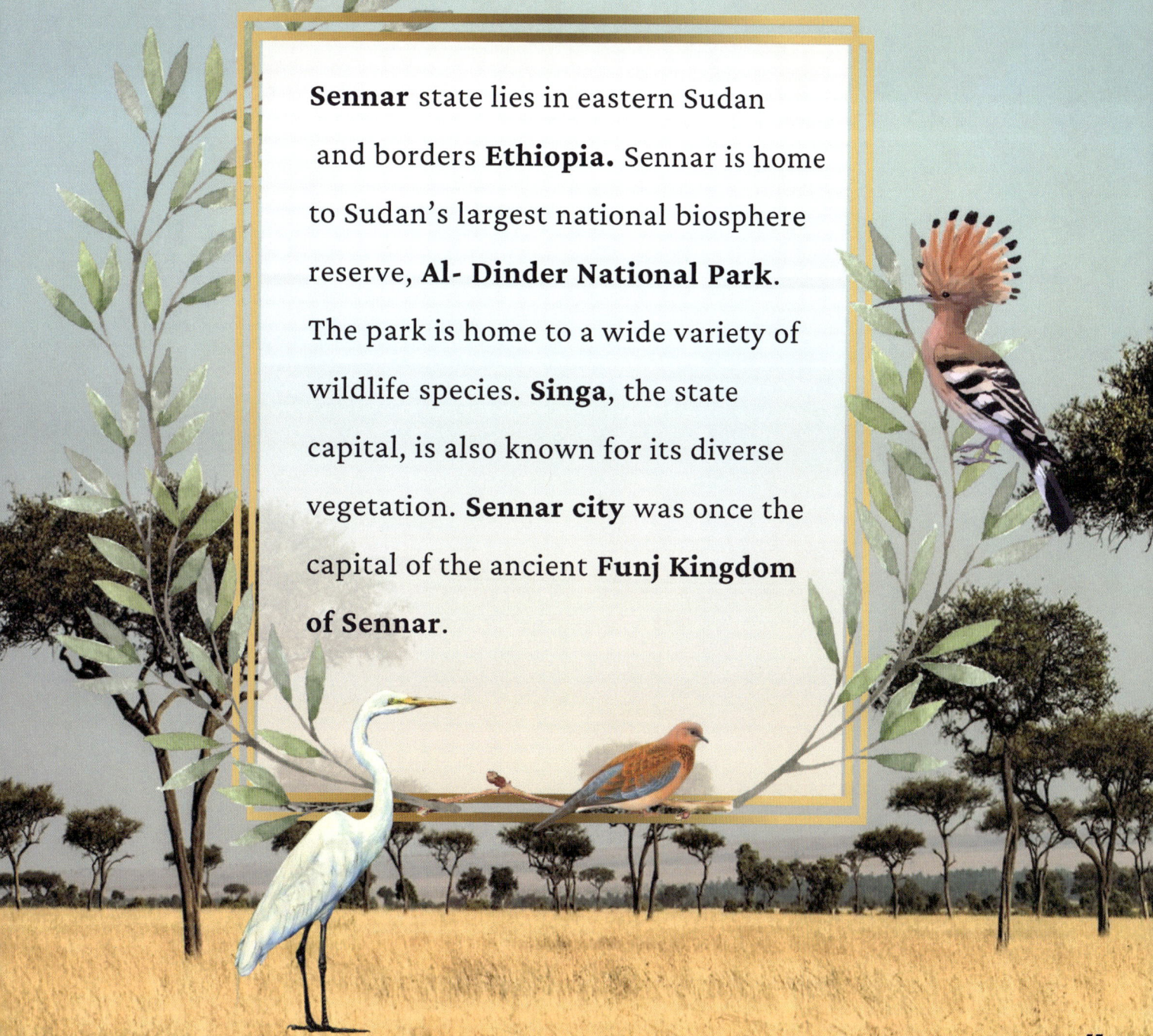

SENNAR STATE

ولاية سنار

Sennar state lies in eastern Sudan and borders **Ethiopia.** Sennar is home to Sudan's largest national biosphere reserve, **Al- Dinder National Park.** The park is home to a wide variety of wildlife species. **Singa**, the state capital, is also known for its diverse vegetation. **Sennar city** was once the capital of the ancient **Funj Kingdom of Sennar.**

SENNAR STATE		ولاية سنار
El-Dinder Reserve		محمية الدندر
El-Dinder River		نهر الدندر
Sennar Dam		خزان سنار
Agriculture		الزراعة

SENNAR STATE

ولاية سنار

Al-Dinder National Park has over 200 species, including cheetahs, leopards, giraffes, fish and reptiles. It is also a central route for migrating birds. **The Dinder River**, a tributary of the **Blue Nile River**, flows through the reserve.

Sennar Dam is located on the **Blue Nile River**. The dam serves in hydraulic power generation and irrigation of agricultural projects. **Al-Suki Agricultural Scheme** is one of the largest agricultural projects in the region.

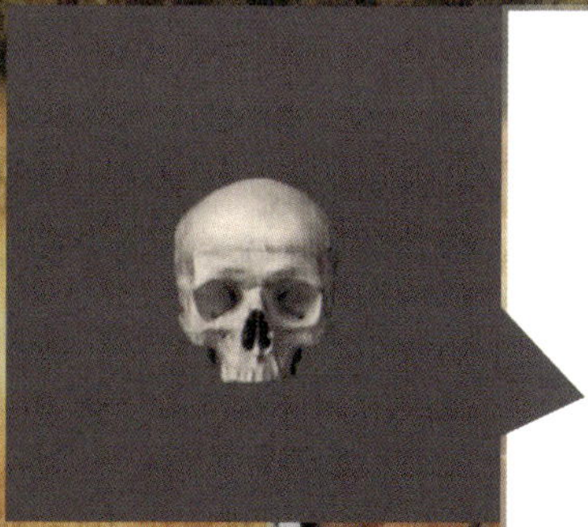

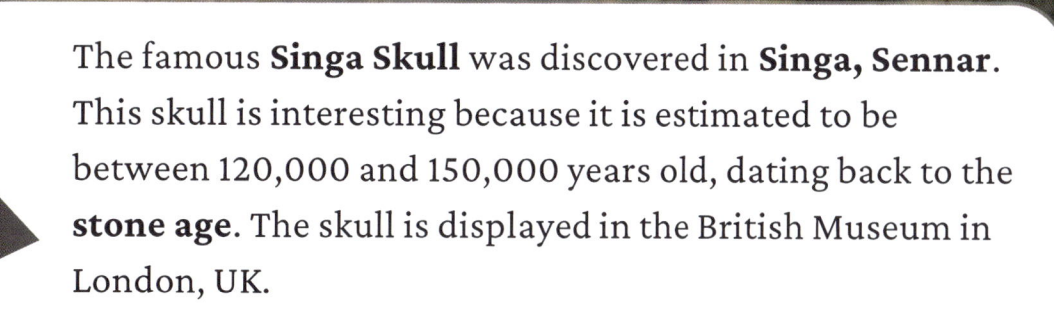

The famous **Singa Skull** was discovered in **Singa, Sennar**. This skull is interesting because it is estimated to be between 120,000 and 150,000 years old, dating back to the **stone age**. The skull is displayed in the British Museum in London, UK.

SENNAR STATE

EXPLORE SUDAN

ولاية سنار

SENNAR STATE

ولاية سنار

WHITE NILE STATE

EXPLORE SUDAN

ولاية النيل الأبيض

Rabak

WHITE NILE STATE

ولاية النيل الأبيض

The **White Nile state** is the center of sugar production in Sudan. The state has vast arable land suited for agriculture. The state capital, **Rabak**, lies on the banks of the **White Nile**. Other notable cities in the state are **Ad Dowiem**, **Al Gutaina** and **Kosti.** The state has many manufacturing companies and fisheries.

WHITE NILE STATE / ولاية النيل الأبيض

Bakhtulreda University	جامعة بخت الرضا
Sugar Production	صناعة السكر
Agriculture	الزراعة
Fisheries	مصائد الأسماك

WHITE NILE STATE

ولاية النيل الأبيض

The renowned **Bakhtulreda University**, in **Ad-Dowiem city**, is known for its pivotal role in promoting education throughout Sudan.

The **White Nile state** is home to Sudan's largest **sugar** factories namely **Kenanah Sugar Company** and **Assalaya Sugar company**.

The **Jebal Aulia Dam** is located on the **White Nile** just south of Khartoum. At the time of its construction in 1937, it was the largest dam in the world. It remains a pivotal source of **hydroelectric power** in Sudan.

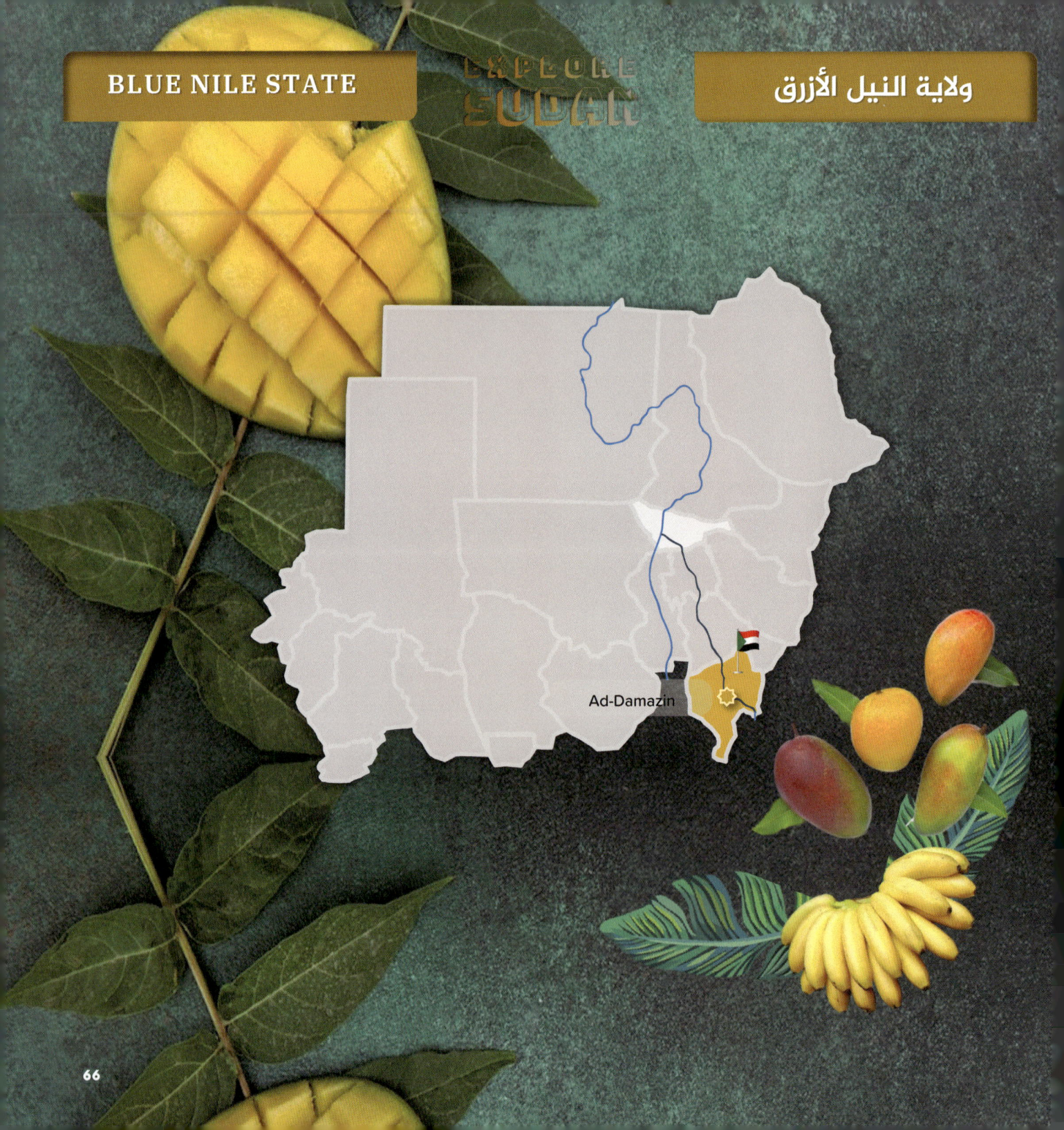

BLUE NILE STATE

ولاية النيل الأزرق

Ad-Damazin

| BLUE NILE STATE | ولاية النيل الأزرق |

The **Blue Nile State** lies south of Khartoum, near the border with **South Sudan**. It has a large **agricultural** sector where a variety of crops are grown including fruits, sorghum, corn, and sunflower.

The state capital, **Ad-Damazin**, is a trading center for crops. The majority of Sudan's local fruit supply comes from the **Blue Nile state** and **Kassala state.**

BLUE NILE STATE / ولاية النيل الأزرق

EXPLORE SUDAN

Roseris Dam	خزان الروصيرص
Roro Mountain	منطقة جبل رورو
Crops	المحاصيل
Fruits	الفواكه
Fisheries	مصائد الأسماك

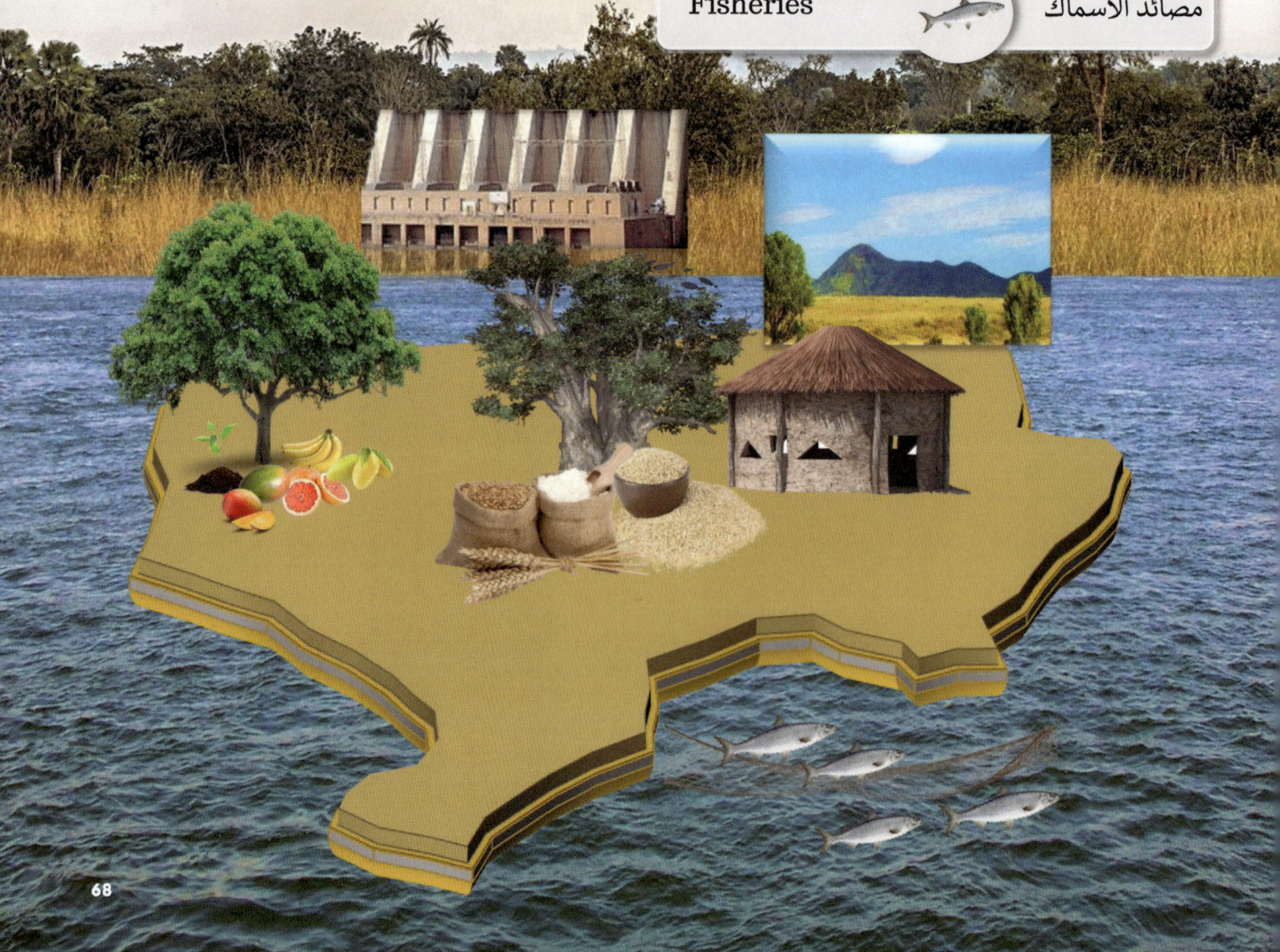

BLUE NILE STATE

ولاية النيل الأزرق

EXPLORE SUDAN

Al-Roseris Dam is located on the Blue Nile. The dam was constructed in 1966 for irrigation and power generation purposes.

Roro Mountain area in the Blue Nile state is known for its beautiful green plains and captivating nature.

The **Blue Nile state** has a large **agricultural** sector where a vast array of crops are grown including **fruits**, **sorghum**, **corn**, and **sunflower**.

KHARTOUM STATE

ولاية الخرطوم

Khartoum

KHARTOUM STATE

EXPLORE SUDAN

ولاية الخرطوم

In Khartoum, the **White Nile** and the **Blue Nile** merge to form the **River Nile**. The area of the confluence of the two rivers known as **Al-Mugran.**

Khartoum is a **tri-capital.** The Nile divides Khartoum state into three distinct cities: **Khartoum**, **Khartoum North** (Bahri) and **Omdurman**. These three cities jointly constitute the national capital of Sudan.

KHARTOUM STATE

ولاية الخرطوم

English	Arabic
Omdurman	أم درمان
Bahri	بحري
Khartoum	الخرطوم

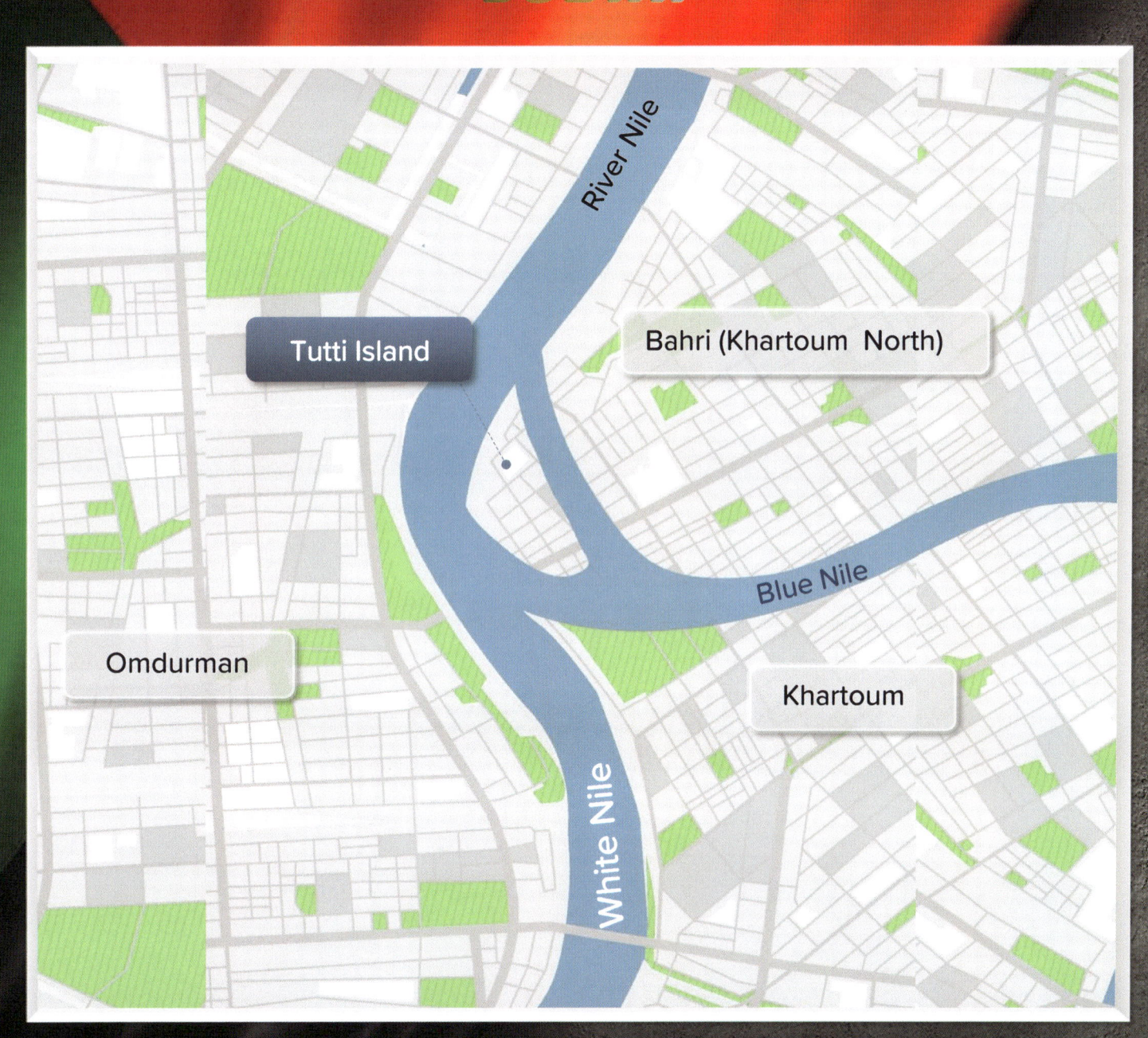

KHARTOUM STATE

ولاية الخرطوم

KHARTOUM CITY

الخرطوم

Khartoum city is the executive capital of Sudan. The majority of municipal buildings are located in Khartoum including the government parliament building.

Other notable landmarks in Khartoum city are the **University of Khartoum**, the **Presidential Palace** and **Sudan's National Museum**.

KHARTOUM CITY

EXPLORE SUDAN

الخرطوم

The Great Mosque
الجامع الكبير

University of Khartoum
جامعة الخرطوم

St. Matthew's Cathedral
كاتدرائية القديس متي

Sudanese National Museum
متحف السودان القومي

The Presidential Palace
القصر الرئاسي

75

BAHRI CITY

EXPLORE SUDAN

بحري

Bahri (Khartoum North) is located north of the **Blue Nile** and east of the River Nile. Bahri is the **industrial center** of the region. It boasts an array of industries including wheat milling, textile production and brick making.

One of the most notable landmarks in Bahri is the **Mosque of Al Sayid Ali Al Merghani**, the leader of the Khatmiya order in Sudan. **Saad Gishra** is Bahri's largest local market and features a large variety of goods.

| BAHRI CITY | EXPLORE SUDAN | بحري |

Al Sayid Ali Al Merghani Mosque

مسجد السيد علي الميرغني

Khartoum Refinery Company Limited

مصفاة الجيلي

Friendship Palace Hotel

فندق قصر الصداقة

OMDURMAN CITY

أم درمان

Omdurman city is the cultural and historic capital of Sudan. The **Tomb of Mohammed Ahmed El Mahdi** and the **Khalifa House Museum** are notable landmarks from the Mahdi era. **Al-Tabya** in Omdurman is one of the defense walls built by the Mahdi during the war.

Sheik Hamad El Nil's tomb and mosque are located in west Omdurman. Here, Sufi dervishes gather to perform their ceremonies and songs. One of the largest markets in the region is **Souq Omdurman**, which exhibits various items including textiles and memorabilia.

OMDURMAN CITY

EXPLORE SUDAN

أم درمان

Al-Nileen Mosque

مسجد النيلين

Tomb of Al-Mahadi

قبر الإمام المهدي

Omdurman Municipal Building

مبنى بلدية أم درمان

Al-Tabya

الطابيه

EXPLORE SUDAN

Resources

EXPLORE SUDAN

- Renewable Energy — الطاقة المتجددة
- Gum Arabic — الصمغ العربي
- Tourism — السياحة
- Agriculture — القطاع الزراعي
- Oil Fields — حقول النفط
- Livestock — الثروة الحيوانية
- Precious Metals — المعادن
- Fisheries — الثروة السمكية

GUM ARABIC

EXPLORE SUDAN

الصمغ العربي

Sudan is the world's **largest exporter of Gum Arabic**. Gum Arabic is a **natural** forest product used extensively in food products. It is an important component of soft drinks, cake icing, candy and chewing gum. Gum Arabic comes from the ***Acacia Senegal and Acacia Seyal*** trees (known locally as Hashab).

The geographic area where the Acacia trees grow is known as the **Gum Arabic belt.** In **Sudan**, the belt stretches from the western border with **Chad** to the eastern border with **Ethiopia**. It covers an area of roughly **500,000 square kilometers**.

USES OF GUM ARABIC

EXPLORE SUDAN

استخدامات الصمغ العربي

- Food — الطعام
- Photography — التصوير
- Color pigments — الأصباغ
- Ceramics — الخزف
- Charcoal — صناعة الفحم
- Adhesive — مادة لاصقة

83

| LIVESTOCK | EXPLORE SUDAN | الثروة الحيوانية |

Camels — الإبل

Sheep — الأغنام

Cows — الأبقار

FISHERIES

EXPLORE SUDAN

الثروة السمكية

Fisheries   مصايد الأسماك

AGRICULTURE — EXPLORE SUDAN — القطاع الزراعي

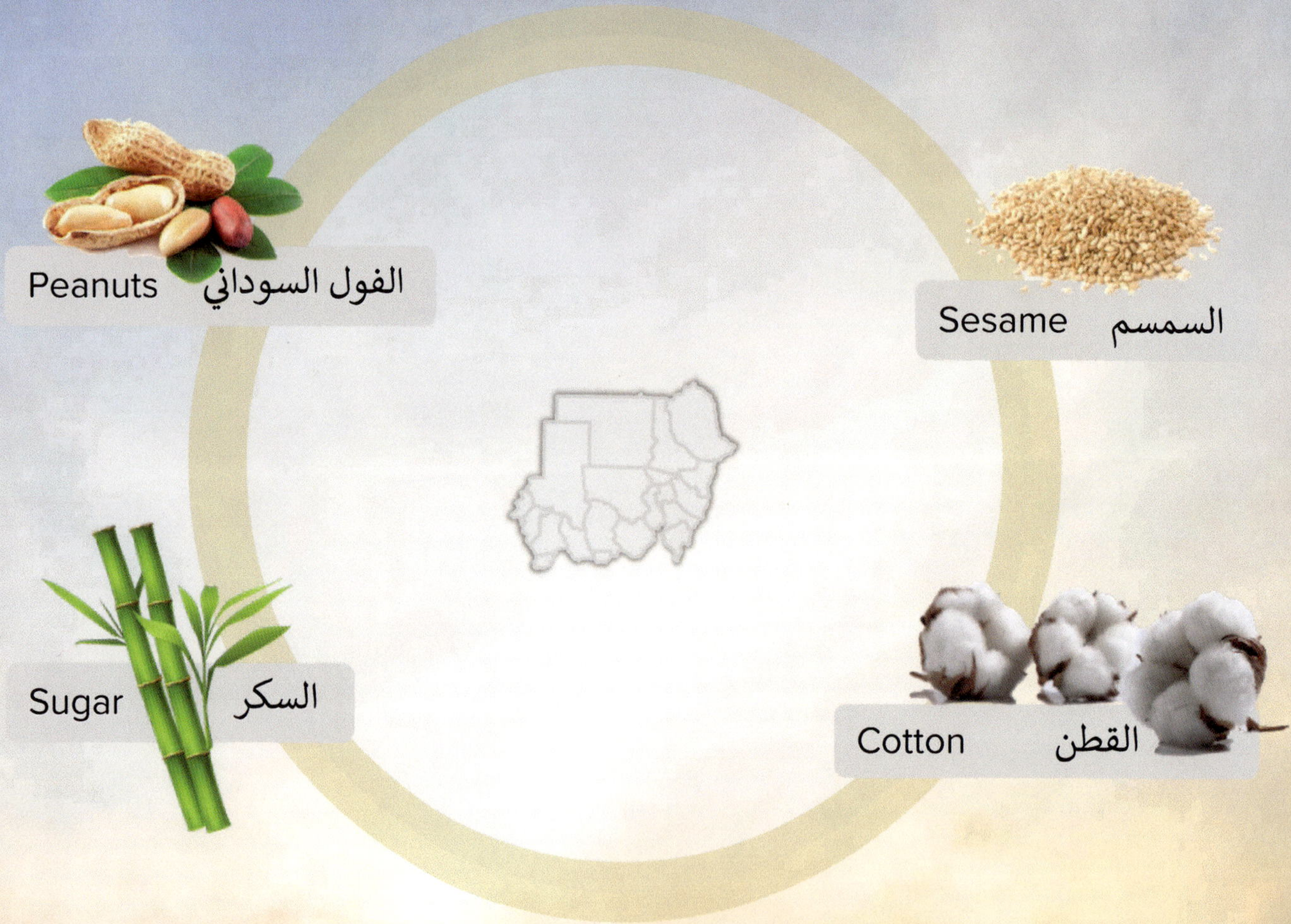

Peanuts — الفول السوداني

Sesame — السمسم

Sugar — السكر

Cotton — القطن

AGRICULTURE

EXPLORE SUDAN

القطاع الزراعي

Sorghum	الذرة الرفيعة
Millet	الدخن
Maize	الذرة
Wheat	القمح

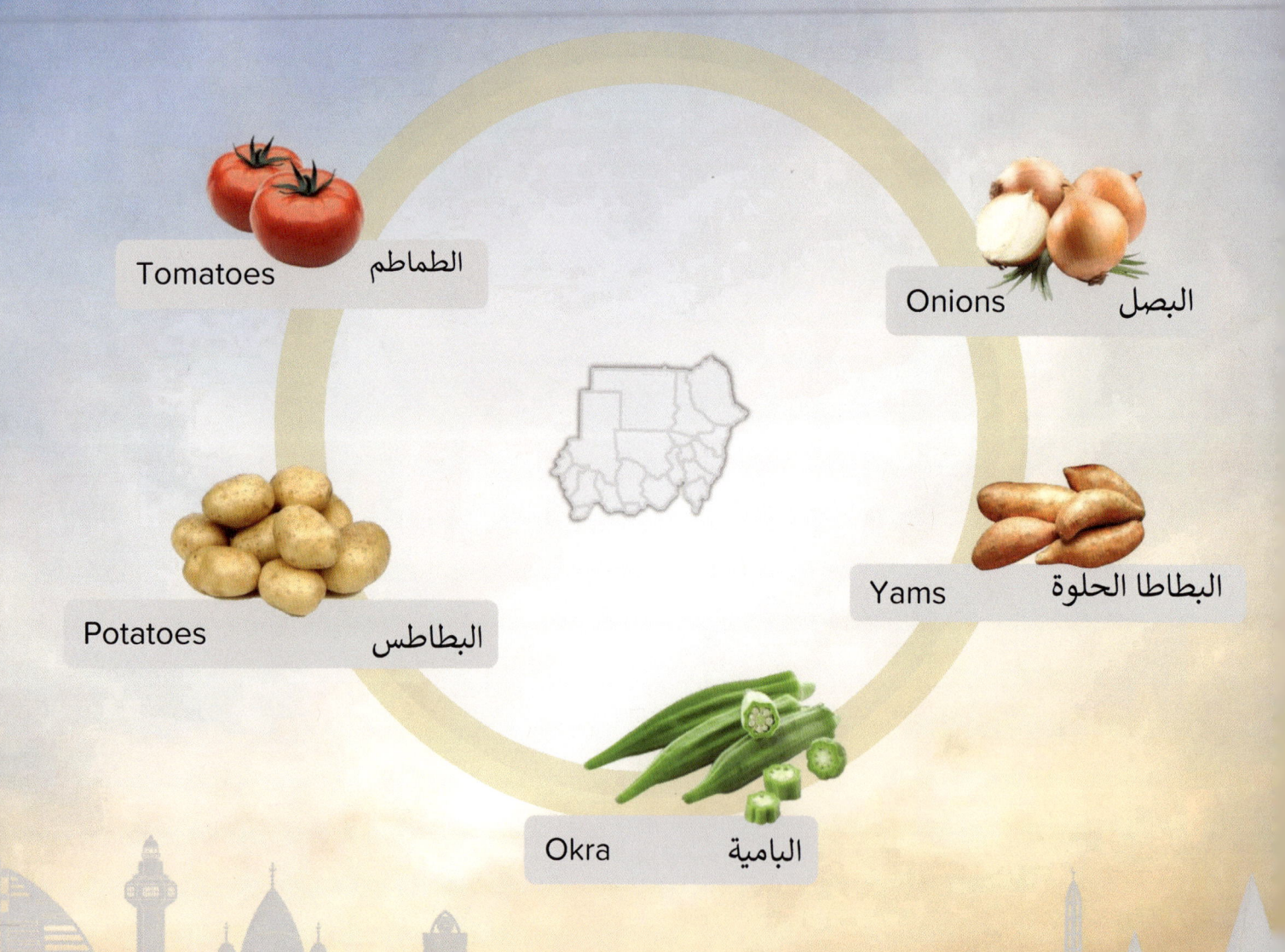

AGRICULTURE

EXPLORE SUDAN

القطاع الزراعي

- Tomatoes — الطماطم
- Onions — البصل
- Potatoes — البطاطس
- Yams — البطاطا الحلوة
- Okra — البامية

AGRICULTURE — EXPLORE SUDAN — القطاع الزراعي

- Hibiscus — الكركديه
- Baobab — القنقليز 
- Doum — الدوم  
- Buckthorn — النبق 
- Balanites Aegyptiaca — اللالوب

AGRICULTURE — EXPLORE SUDAN — القطاع الزراعي

- Citrus Fruits — الحمضيات
- Dates — التمر
- Mangoes — المنجا
- Watermelon — البطيخ
- Bananas — الموز

MINERALS — التعدين

EXPLORE SUDAN

Copper	النحاس
Gold	الذهب
Iron ore	خام الحديد
Silver	الفضة
Chromium	الكروم
Asbestos	الاسبست
Uranium	اليورانيوم

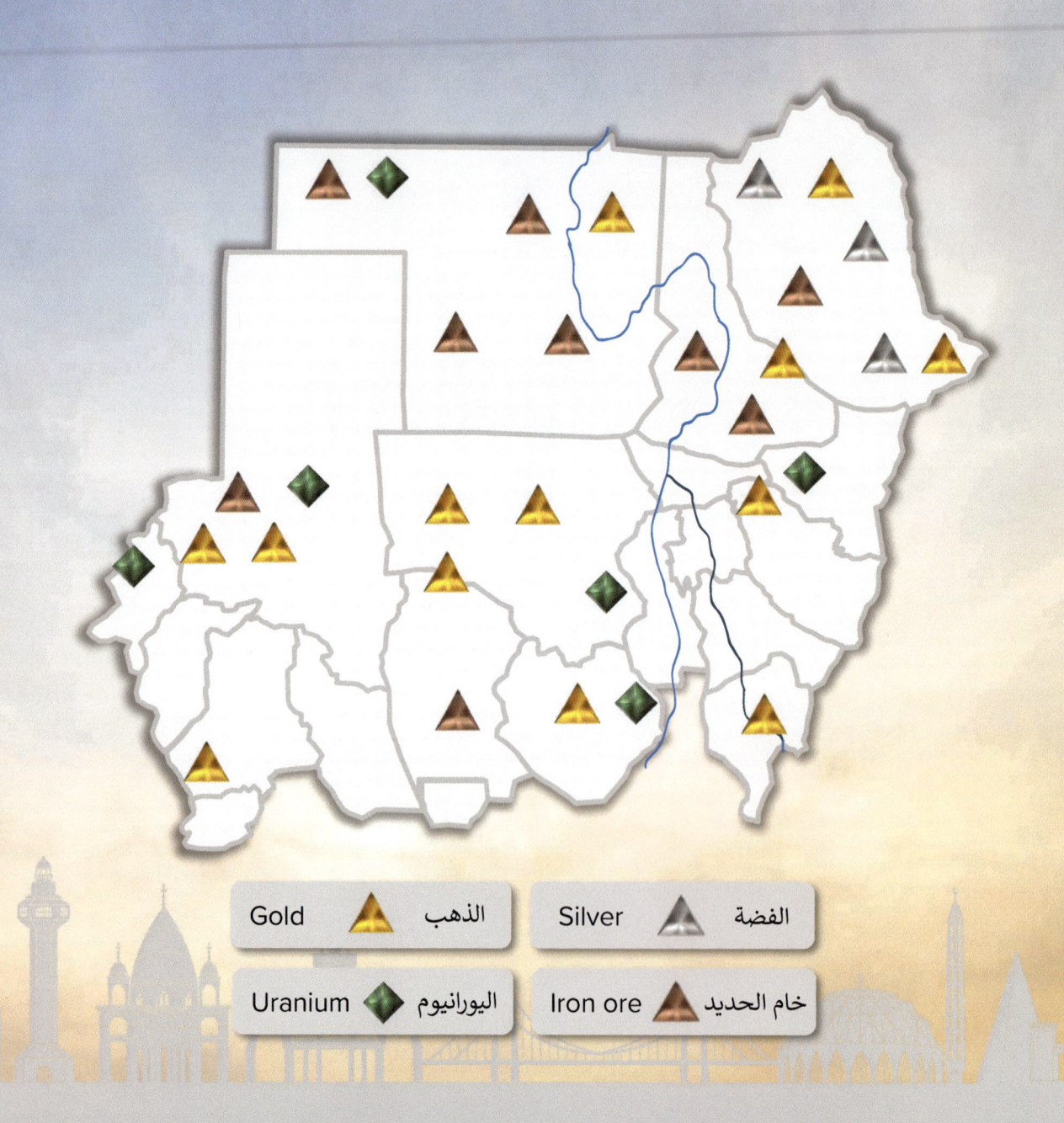

MINERALS — EXPLORE SUDAN — التعدين

| Gold — الذهب | Silver — الفضة |
| Uranium — اليورانيوم | Iron ore — خام الحديد |

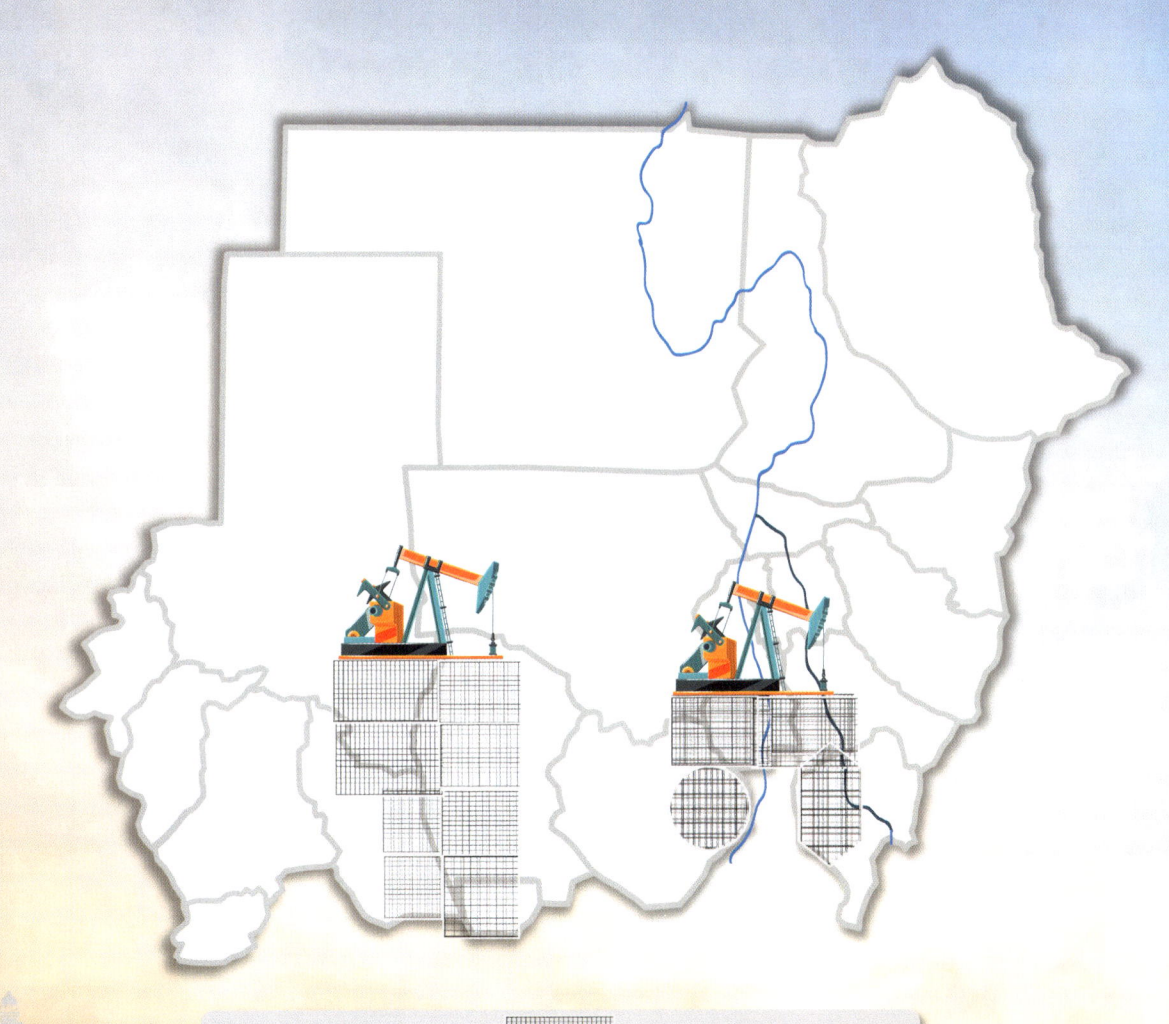

OIL FIELDS

EXPLORE SUDAN

حقول النفط

| Oil Fields | حقول النفط |

TOURISM   **EXPLORE SUDAN**   السياحة

TOURISM

EXPLORE SUDAN

السياحة

Al Bagrawiyah — البجراوية

Jebel Barkal — جبل البركل

اهرامات جبل البركل
Pyramids of Jebel Barkal

متحف علي دينار
Ali Dinar Museum

Nuri — نوري

Old Dongola — دنقلا العجوز

95

| TOURISM | EXPLORE **SUDAN** | السياحة |

96

| RENEWABLE ENERGY | EXPLORE SUDAN | الطاقة المتجددة |

Hydropower — الطاقة الكهرمائية

Wind Energy — طاقة الرياح

Solar Energy — الطاقة الشمسية

WIND ENERGY — EXPLORE SUDAN — طاقة الرياح

According to United Nations Development Program, wind conditions in Sudan are very favorable for electricity generation.

The regions with the highest potential are north **Darfur**, the **Northern State** and along the **Red Sea coast.**

In these areas, the monthly average of **wind speeds** are very favorable for electricity generation, **reaching up to 8 m/s.**

WIND ENERGY

EXPLORE SUDAN

طاقة الرياح

SOLAR ENERGY

EXPLORE SUDAN

الطاقة الشمسية

Sudan has immense potential in exploiting **solar energy** mainly due to its **geographic location**. The average sunshine duration ranges from **8.5 to 11 hours per day**.

The map on the right shows the **Solar power map** of Sudan, based on the World Bank's Solar Atlas.

The annual average solar radiation in Sudan exceeds 2000 kWh/m2, which is among the highest in the world.

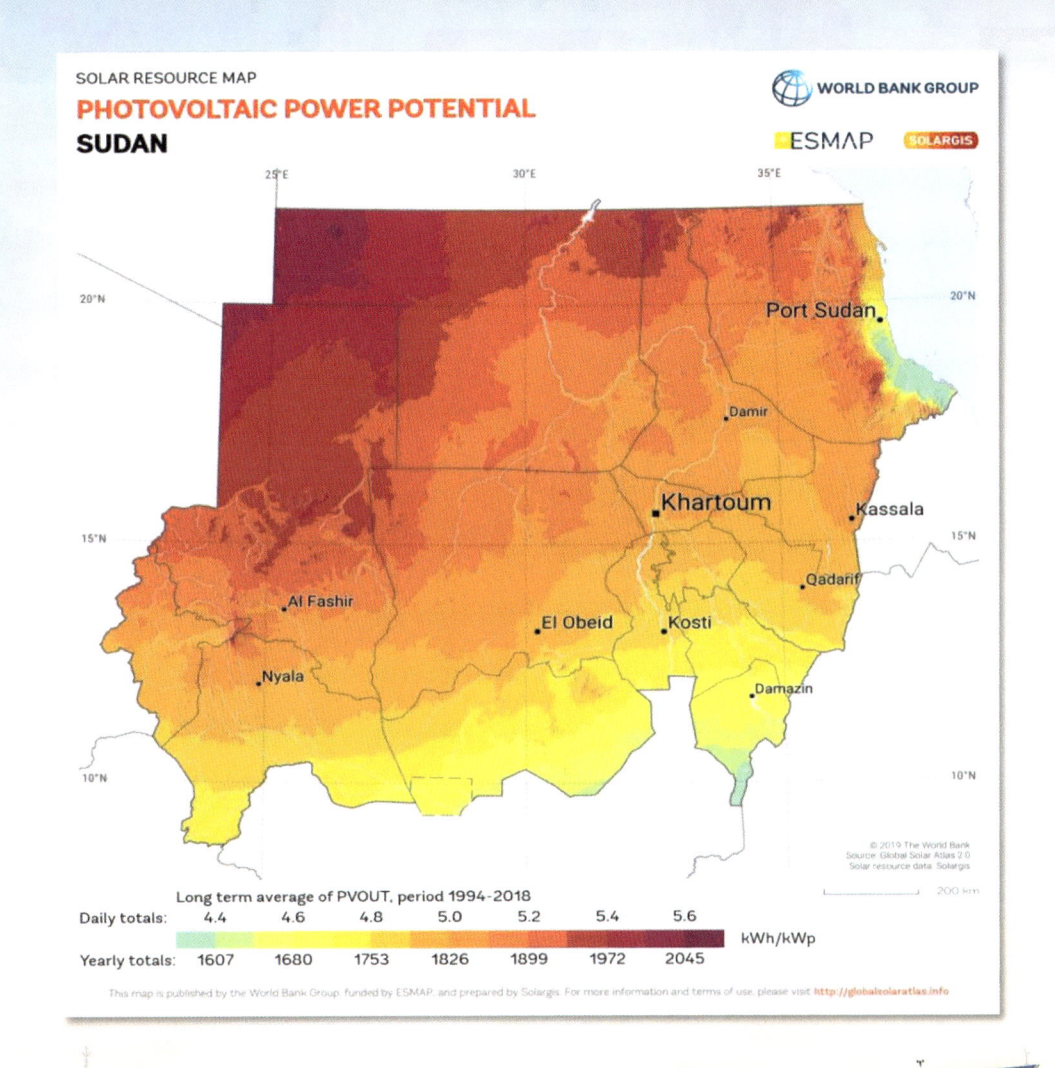

SOLAR ENERGY

EXPLORE SUDAN

الطاقة الشمسية

SOLAR RESOURCE MAP
PHOTOVOLTAIC POWER POTENTIAL
SUDAN

Long term average of PVOUT, period 1994-2018

Daily totals:	4.4	4.6	4.8	5.0	5.2	5.4	5.6	kWh/kWp
Yearly totals:	1607	1680	1753	1826	1899	1972	2045	

This map is published by the World Bank Group, funded by ESMAP, and prepared by Solargis. For more information and terms of use, please visit http://globalsolaratlas.info

© 2019 The World Bank
Source: Global Solar Atlas 2.0
Solar resource data: Solargis

HYDROPOWER

EXPLORE SUDAN

الطاقة الكهرمائية

Sennar Dam — خزان سنار

Roseris Dam — خزان الروصيرص

Jebal Aulia Dam — خزان جبل أولياء

Meroe Dam — خزان مروي

EXPLORE SUDAN

The End

References   EXPLORE SUDAN   المراجع

1. USAID, WFP, & FEWS NET. (2011). Livelihoods Zoning "plus" Activity In Sudan A Special Report By The Famine Early Warning Systems Network Retrieved May 16, 2021 from https://documents.wfp.org/stellent/groups/public/documents/ena/wfp239943.pdf

2. Ranganathan, R. & Briceño-Garmendia, C. (2011) Sudan's Infrastructure: A Continental Perspective. World Bank, Washington, DC. Retrieved May 16, 2021 from https://openknowledge.worldbank.org/handle/10986/27270

3. The Ministry of Environment & Higher Council for Environment and Natural Resources. (2016) Republic of The Sudan National Adaptation Plan Retrieved from https://www4.unfccc.int/sites/NAPC/Documents NAP/National Reports/Sudan NAP.pdf

4. FAO (2013) Food security Technical Secretariat (FSTS) | Blue Nile State Food Security Technical Secretariat (FSTS) Market Trends and Performance of 2013 Agricultural Season. Retrieved from https://coin.fao.org/coin-static/cms/media/20/13986652001280/bn_first_fs_bulletin-.pdf

5. Food and Agriculture Organization of the United Nations | Livelihoods of small-scale fishers along the Nile River in Sudan | Inland Fisheries Retrieved May 16, 2021, from http://www.fao.org/inland-fisheries/topics/detail/en/c/1146874/

6. D Nasr (2015) Dungonab Bay/Mukawar Island Area (SUDAN) An Ecologically Significant Marine Area.

7. Sudan Ministry of Energy & Oil | Map Exploration Retrieved May 16, 2021, from http://www.mop.gov.sd/eng/page/map

8. The Geological Research Authority of Sudan (GRAS) & The Republic of the Sudan Ministry of Minerals. The Next Major Gold Mining Destination In Africa- Retrieved May 16, 2021 from https://www.cgs.gov.cn/ddztt/kydh/2017kydh/kjcx/201709/P020170921524008422172.pdf

9. Hassai Gold Mine – Red Sea Project Retrieved May 16, 2021 from https://www.mining-technology.com/projects/hassai-mine/

References | المراجع

10. Pantuliano, S., Assal, M., Elnaiem, B. A., Mcelhinney, H., Schwab, M., Elzein, Y., Saeed, R. (2011). City limits: urbanisation and vulnerability in Sudan Khartoum case study Research team. Retrieved May 16, 2021 from www.odi.org.uk/hpg

11. Sanganeb Atoll, Sudan A Marine National Park with Scientific Criteria for Ecologically Significant Marine Areas. Retrieved May 16, 2021 from https://www.cbd.int/doc/meetings/mar/ebsaws-2015-02/other/ebsaws-2015-02-template-sudan-01-en.pdf

12. UNESCO Sanganeb Marine National Park and Dungonab Bay – Mukkawar Island Marine National Park - UNESCO World Heritage Centre. Accessed May 16, 2021, from https://whc.unesco.org/en/list/262/

13. Spaulding, Jay L., Unit, Economist Intelligence, Sikainga, Ahmad Alawad, Sabr, Mohy el Din, Collins, Robert O. and Al-Shahi, Ahmed S.. "Sudan". Encyclopedia Britannica, 10 Mar. 2021, Accessed May 16, 2021 from https://www.britannica.com/place/Sudan

14. Sudan – Wikipedia https://en.wikipedia.org/wiki/Sudan Accessed Apri 12, 2020

15. Hassabelgabo, S., Ibrahim, A., Shukri, M. I., & Agab, E. B. (2020). Review of the Updated Status, Potentials and Renewable Energies Plans in Sudan. International Research Journal of Engineering and Technology. Retrieved from www.irjet.net

16. Renewable Energy in Sudan: Status and Potential - Part 1 - Renewables in Africa. (n.d.). Retrieved May 18, 2021, from https://www.renewablesinafrica.com/renewable-energy-in-sudan-status-and-potential-part-1/

17. Saeed, T. M., Bashier, E., Tayeb, M., & Osman, G. (2019). Sustainable Energy Potential in Sudan. SUST Journal of Engineering and Computer Sciences (JECS) (Vol. 02).

18. Sudan, UNDP invest in wind energy | REVE News of the wind sector in Spain and in the world. (n.d.). Retrieved May 19, 2021, from https://www.evwind.es/2014/12/08/sudan-undp-invest-in-wind-energy/49325

PHOTO CREDITS

EXPLORE SUDAN

مصادر الصور

Page 21 Jebel Marrah Picture By Hammy07, CC BY-SA 3.0,
https://commons.wikimedia.org/w/index.php?curid=1557111

Page 22 Nuba Mountains Picture By Andreas31 - (C) Andreas31, CC BY-SA 3.0,
https://commons.wikimedia.org/w/index.php?curid=473746

Page 31 Nuri Picture By Vit Hassan - originally posted to Flickr as Monuments CC BY-SA 2.0,
https://commons.wikimedia.org/w/index.php?curid=63076711

Page 42 Port Sudan Picture By Bertramz - Own work, CC BY 3.0,
https://commons.wikimedia.org/w/index.php?curid=5654739

Page 47 Kassala Picture by Bertramz, CC BY 3.0 <https://creativecommons.org/licenses/by/3.0>,
via Wikimedia Commons

Page 47 Khatmiya Mosque Picture By Bertramz, CC BY 3.0 <https://creativecommons.org/licenses/by/3.0>,
via Wikimedia Commons

Page 59 Sennar Dam Picture By Mussapedia - Own work, CC BY-SA 3.0,
https://commons.wikimedia.org/w/index.php?curid=25058703

Page 69 Roseiris Dam Picture By SimonChilly - Own work, CC BY 3.0,
https://commons.wikimedia.org/w/index.php?curid=19134616

EXPLORE SUDAN

- 🐦 @explore_sudan
- **Explore Sudan Book Series** @exploresudanbooks
- 📷 @ExploreSudanBooks

Printed in Great Britain
by Amazon